# The Last Flight of
# Bert Hinkler

## Edward P. Wixted

**VANTAGE PRESS**
New York

Copyright © 1992 by Edward P. Wixted

Published by Vantage Press, Inc.
516 West 34th Street, New York, New York 10001

Manufactured in the United States of America
ISBN: 0-533-09021-0

Library of Congress Catalog Card No.: 90-90049

1 2 3 4 5 6 7 8 9 0

To

Thomas Michael Wixted
22 November 1889–15 October 1958

and

the search for truth

# CONTENTS

# AUTHORISATIONS AND ACKNOWLEDGEMENTS

The author accepts full responsibility for the facts and conclusions presented in *The Last Flight of Bert Hinkler*.

Bert Hinkler's brothers, Jack and George, and his sister, Queenie, lent their authority at different points in time to assist enquiries that became necessary. The relatives of persons who are named in the text as Nancy and Katherine did not avail themselves of the opportunity to assist.

Elucidation, or confirmation, of purely historical facts was assisted by:

L. A. Cordingley
Steve Brogden
Jim Laver
A. Crosthwaite
John B. S. Savage
Kevin Lindeberg, whose enquiries in Italy were greatly facilitated
    by
Amedeo di Savoia, duke of Aosta, and
Luciano Centini

## CREDITS

Photographs have been credited on the basis of information available to the author. Where information as to origins is unclear, or where multiple copies are known to be in existence, the photographs are unattributed. Newspaper reports of the 1932–33 period are reproduced in confirmation of statements in the text as to the content of those reports, or of attitudes that the author knows to have been held at that time but which otherwise lack a suitable documentary basis. The source of certain other material, such as letters, has not been indicated as a matter of deliberate practice, given the nature of the conclusions presented.

For permission to reproduce items from the 1933 press thanks are due to Times Newspapers Ltd., (publishers of *The Times*); John Fairfax Group Pty. Ltd. (*Sydney Morning Herald*); Davies Brothers Ltd. (Hobart *Mercury*); Queensland Newspapers Pty. Ltd., (*Courier, Sunday Mail, Daily Mail*); Bundaberg Newspaper Co. Pty. Ltd. (*Bundaberg Daily News and Mail*); Guardian Newspapers Ltd. (*Manchester Guardian*); Reed Business Publishing Group (*Flight International, Aeroplane Monthly*); La Nazione (specifically journalists Alfredo Bennati, 1933, and Giulio Giustiniani, 1974); *Southern Evening Echo*; and the London *Daily Mail*.

A number of other 1933 newspapers are no longer published.

## ASSISTANCE

Almost all enquiries and requests met with extensive cooperation. The cooperation took diverse forms.Some acknowledgements will be found in the text and in the inscriptions accompanying photographs.

During a crucial period, Jean and George Cull rendered assistance on a personal level that was particularly valued. Howard Kingsford, a former sectional airworthiness surveyor, was always prepared to discuss aspects of aeronautical engineering. Liberata Burman's assistance with Italian correspondence and documents contributed greatly to progress in the early period of investigations.

Professional and technical advice from Ms. Kathy Buckley and David Bligh greatly simplified the task of finalising the text and improving the presentation of illustrations. Vynette McKenzie tested the practicability of several presentation ideas with useful results. Rasjad Moore examined the text closely and made several useful suggestions.

Bert Hinkler and his aircraft

*Jim Laver*

# SQN. LDR. H.J.L. HINKLER, AFC, DSM
## 1892–1933

Australia's pioneers of flying concede pride of place to no one. They stand shoulder to shoulder on the world stage with the greatest from other nations including America's Charles Lindbergh. This may surprise Americans. Among pioneer aviators of the then British Empire no one stands taller, despite his shortness of physical stature, than Bert Hinkler.

Bert Hinkler was one of aviation's foremost achievers. His pioneering flights were inspirational. There were others among his flying compatriots of the 1920s and 1930s who, like Hinkler, became household names in many parts of the British Empire. They helped consolidate the feeling for an Australian national identity first forged on the battlefields in 1914–1918. Their fame lives on.

Bert Hinkler first rose to prominence with a flight described by the *Aeroplane* as "the most meritorious flight on record": his London–Turin flight over the Alps in a light biplane in 1920. Honours and fame accumulated: a London to Latvia flight in 1927; the pioneering solo flight from England to Australia in 1928; piloting the first Canadian aircraft to arrive in Britain under its own power in 1931. In the course of the 1931 flight he won himself a place in the aviation history of Canada, the U.S.A., the West Indies, the Caribbean, Venezuela and Brazil.

In this book you will become aware of Hinkler's achievements progressively, but the initial focus of attention is on his last flight. The reader who feels a need for greater introductory knowledge of Hinkler might like to consult Appendix 2 first.

Three of Australia's foremost airmen lost their lives in successive years—Hinkler in 1933, Charles Ulm off Hawaii in 1934, and Sir Charles Kingsford Smith off the coast of Burma in 1935. Neither Ulm nor Kingsford Smith was ever found. Bert Hinkler was making an England–Australia flight (with the intention of continuing on to Canada) when he met his tragic end. The flight ended in Italy, far short of even his initial destination. This book examines the strange circumstances surrounding the death of this famous airman.

# The Last Flight
# of Bert Hinkler

# BRIEFING

On 7 January 1933, Bert Hinkler left a London aerodrome on a flight to Australia. The flight was destined to be his last. Earth and sky swallowed him up, and it was almost four months before anything further was heard or seen of him. High on an Apennine mountainside, after the melting of the snows, an Italian carbon collector caught a glimpse of a large white object of unnatural shape. Hinkler's wrecked Puss Moth aircraft had at last been discovered. Nearby was the body of the pilot.

The Bert Hinkler story did not end there. A memorial was erected on the spur overlooking the site, and in the course of time, in Australia and elsewhere, other memorials were added. Interest in Hinkler's pioneering aviation achievements continues unabated. In 1969 the aviation magazine *Flight International* nominated Bert Hinkler as one of the twelve immortals of all-time aviation. In the 1988 Australian Bicentenary celebrations a major air race was named in his honour.

How and why did Hinkler crash? He had often experienced weather much worse than that which prevailed on the day of his disappearance. Thirteen months earlier he had flown the South Atlantic in the same aircraft and come safely through a fierce Atlantic gale.

The official version of the crash said that Hinkler's aircraft lost a wing in midair. The evidence of eye witnesses who arrived earliest at the mountainside crash scene shows this to be erroneous. The wing was found on the mountain slope beside the tree that knocked it off.

Close examination of all the evidence reveals that the skilled flyer—Hinkler had once been chief test pilot for the Avro Company—crashed when attempting an emergency landing following the loss of a blade of his propeller during flight. Strong winds and downdraughts prevail in the mountainous region where Hinkler was forced down. Disaster followed his landing attempt.

The loss of a propeller blade in flight is unusual, and the state of the fallen aircraft requires explanation. A "blade retention failure" was unknown to the U.S. manufacturer. The uniqueness of the circumstance raises the possibility of tampering as one explanation. The engine would have been pulled from its mountings if the blade had separated from the propeller assembly while the engine was at normal revolutions. It seems Hinkler received some warning as the problem developed.

Had Bert Hinkler been successful in his emergency landing attempt or had he survived the crash that followed, there would have been little he could have done, even then, to sheet home [prove] responsibility for the propeller condition. To the uninformed any attempt by Hinkler to do so would have seemed like "sour grapes" on his part.

However, the prolonged period of Hinkler's disappearance while his fate remained unknown brought onto the stage the various characters who played roles in the drama of his final flight. From the conduct of a small group it is certain that they acted on the basis of an organised, and prior, expectation that Hinkler would not survive the flight.

A veil of secrecy, misconception, and deception concealed the true position in 1933. The two versions of Hinkler's last flight to become accepted—the official version that his plane lost a wing in midair and fell to earth and the publicly accepted version that Hinkler took off in very bad weather from an aerodrome at Feltham in England, told no one where he was going, and crashed more than twelve hours later into a mountain in Italy during a snowstorm—were not consistent with the facts. Apart from factual errors both require the blind acceptance of unexplained peculiarities and inconsistencies. Several such features were present, unnoticed at the time, in photographs of the crash published in 1933 and then later, on the Australian scene, in those published on the front page of *Smith's Weekly* on 5 September 1936. A hidden mystery attached to Bert Hinkler's last flight, and the elements that would finally unravel the mystery were dispersed throughout five countries—England, Italy, Canada, the U.S.A., and Australia.

The process of unravelling the mystery did not commence initially from the idea that Bert Hinkler had suffered foul play.

That suspicion, when it did occur, came suddenly and uninvited. From that point onwards enquiries were carried out on a systematic basis. That which seemed at the initial moment of insight to be the real explanation was tested by endeavouring to prove it incorrect. This served only to confirm its accuracy and brought to light unexpected information. Several of the author's closer associates played significant roles in these enquiries. As might be expected, however, many enquiries met a wall of silence throughout.

That the evidence gathered during these enquiries did not become the basis of an official investigation cannot be laid at my door. My requests for official action were ignored by authorities in Australia and England. Official action would have resolved the mystery during the lifetime of the persons concerned, perhaps through the courts. Even more importantly, minimal action by government authorities could have provided each of the three persons with the opportunity of speaking on their own account and stating their own position in respect to the matters of substance at the centre of enquiries. Whether those concerned would have welcomed the opportunity is a moot point; that such an opportunity was denied them is the responsibility of others. I eventually interviewed the last survivor with the unusual, but not unexpected, result recorded in Chapter 12.

The investigation was a search for truth and I accept complete responsibility for my conclusions.

It is often the case that truth can be hurtful. I am conscious that relatives of some of the persons referred to—and perhaps, too, present occupants of some long-standing official positions—may feel injured by this publication, but the story as I have here presented it must now be told. No other course could be contemplated. The stature of Hinkler as a national and international figure is insistent that the facts be stated.

A wealth of first-hand evidence has been consulted; eye witnesses have been interviewed. This will be readily apparent to the attentive reader, as also will be the fact that much original source material has not been identified as such within the text. The reason for this procedure will be evident upon reflection. There is in existence, in manuscript form, a much larger version of *The Last Flight of Bert Hinkler*, one which is fully documented.

The author is not dependent upon news reports for his information. Such reports, where they appear, are a record of what was stated, or known, publicly during the significant period.

The reader is introduced to the events surrounding Bert Hinkler's final flight. The sequence in which the story is told is designed to embark the reader upon his own voyage of discovery, not only about the circumstances of the final flight, but about Hinkler himself as a man. To minimise distractions, much detail has been removed to the Appendices: this information should be considered an essential part of the story.

A generation accustomed to intercontinental airline services as an everyday fact of life, that can make almost instantaneous accommodation bookings in far-off places at the press of computer keys, then arrive at that accommodation within twenty-four hours, may experience difficulty with the atmosphere of the pioneering years of aviation and communication. In those days big ocean liners, passenger ships, crammed the ports of the world. There was no television, no satellite communication. Wireless, the daily newspaper, and later, newsreels shown in movie theatres brought the news of the world to the public. The minds of the people did not have to cope with the clutter that came with the proliferation of the media. Issues and events lodged in the mind. No "air mail," in a hemispheric sense, existed. No commercial airliners crossed the Atlantic or the Pacific. Photographs, if they were to be published in an overseas country, had to be carried there physically.

The sky was uncrowded. A handful of brave, resolute, and apparently diffident aviators set standards of endurance and speed as they rivalled each other in long-distance flights. When they took off from an airfield, they literally took off into the blue. It was the day of the sky kings.

Men still alive today lived through that period and participated in its events. Others, of a not too-considerable age, recall the era and its atmosphere. In its own time the death of Bert Hinkler, and men like him, changed the nature of their world.

# 1
# JANUARY 1933

Where the mellow light from the hangar merged with the darkness of the airfield, three men stood talking together. As they separated a few last words punctuated their movements. Two of the men walked to nearby cars. Their companion turned back towards the hangar. He was small in stature and even in the dim light it was clear he was attired for flight with helmet, gloves, and flying coat. The airman walked towards a solitary figure who stood quietly watching proceedings. This man was the airfield caretaker and his name was Harris. A short distance away the engine of a Puss Moth monoplane filled the night with sound. The engine had been switched on when the aircraft was wheeled from the hangar and was now warming up. Its noise made conversation difficult. As the caretaker and airman met, there was a brief discussion between them. Then they shook hands. "And thank Mrs. Harris for looking after me, too," the airman concluded. Harris nodded and said, "Good luck."

It was a cold winter's night. Bert Hinkler was about to take off from a London aerodrome on a flight to Australia. He entered the cabin of the aircraft and pulled the door shut. As Harris removed the chocks from the wheels, the engine noise increased to a high-pitched whine. The Puss Moth gradually eased forward towards the grass. Hinkler had waited a long time for this moment, months in fact. He had hoped to be in Australia long before winter arrived in England, but there had been frustrating delays. Installing a new Gipsy Major engine in place of the previous Gipsy III had caused part of the delay but only a small part. Its extra power would more than justify itself on the long flight ahead. Now, in the early morning hours of Saturday, 7 January 1933, it seemed nothing more could stand in his way. But even during this same night a mist settling on the aerodrome had forced a slight change in Hinkler's departure arrangements.

The Puss Moth moved off towards the southeast corner of the aerodrome and disappeared from view. The airman's two companions were already out on the airfield with their cars positioned. The Great West Aerodrome provided plenty of space for a long takeoff run, but there were no facilities for aerial activity after nightfall. The car lights would help guide Hinkler once he accelerated for takeoff. When Hinkler reached his starting point near the southeast corner, he swung his aircraft around into the wind. As he did so a mist descended and blanketed the whole airfield. Throughout the next forty minutes the only sound heard by the waiting men was the distant hum of the aircraft engine.

With the same suddenness the mist lifted. The roar of the engine increased. Jack Savage and Dopey Lingham, their car lights illuminating the runway, took a renewed interest in events. The heavily loaded Puss Moth in all probability would use most of the available space. They could sense the aircraft approaching. Lingham briefly glimpsed the ghostly outline of the Puss Moth as it passed in the moonlight above, already more than twenty feet off the ground and climbing, a spark descending from its exhaust. It was 3:10 A.M. The two men listened but when it was clear Bert Hinkler was on his way and did not intend the customary circuit of the aerodrome, they returned to their vehicles and drove off.

The Fairey Aviation Company owned the Great West Aerodrome at Heath Row and throughout the long wait the company's ambulance had been manned and in readiness. It returned to its station as Savage and Lingham left the aerodrome.

Alone in his aircraft Hinkler set a course for Paris and whatever might lie beyond. He had every reason to feel satisfied with himself. All his preparations had been completed methodically and his last day in England, Friday, 6 January, had given him the satisfaction of calling on a number of old friends. No doubt the long series of incidents so recently experienced lingered in Hinkler's mind and tumbled about, triggering other thoughts as his aircraft flew steadily through the darkness towards France.

One of the friends Hinkler had visited was C. G. Grey, editor of a long-established aviation magazine, the *Aeroplane*. Bert Hinkler had arrived in England as a young man in 1914, and he had known Grey almost since that time. The magazine, which really meant Grey himself, had always given sympathetic support to Hinkler's various aviation ventures, and the friendship was long-standing. Another friend Hinkler had called on was L. H. Pike, an official representative of the Queensland government in London. Their friendship was of several years duration. In 1928 Hinkler had won great renown with his pioneering solo flight from England to Australia and it had been Pike who afterwards made the arrangements for the aircraft Hinkler used on that flight, an Avro Avian biplane, to be donated by the airman to the Queensland government.

Hinkler had also flown down from Hendon to Southampton on that last day in England to attend a luncheon organised in his honour by the Hampshire Aero Club. In the main it was a gathering of flying men, but there were others in Southampton with whom Hinkler had connections of a more personal nature. Hinkler's long-standing friend, Jim Laver, worked for the Union Castle Line, and Hinkler had called on him at his office near Southampton Water. Laver was at once greeted by Hinkler with the remark, "I'm leaving tomorrow, Jim, and I've come to say goodbye." They left the office and had coffee and a bun together. After they parted at the Floating Bridge, a vehicle and passenger ferry linking the city with the districts south of the Itchen River, Hinkler made for Hamble Aerodrome and Jim Laver returned to his office.

By three o'clock in the afternoon Hinkler had arrived back in London from Hamble. He landed at Croydon. He remained at Croydon for an hour while Customs formalities were completed then flew across the city to the Great West Aerodrome at Heath Row, near Harmondsworth. After he landed at 4:15 P.M., he reported back to Croydon by telephone, then supervised the refuelling of his aircraft. When a telephone call came he declined to take it because the refuelling was still in progress. The call was from Joe Taylor. A well-known airman in earlier days, Taylor was now the aviation officer for Shell Mex. The gallonage taken on by the Puss Moth was essential information for his company for drawback purposes with the Customs. Refuelling having been completed, Hinkler contacted him at 5:17 P.M. After speaking to Taylor, Hinkler telephoned Croydon again.

Two hours remained before dinner, which was set for 7:30 P.M. It was being prepared by Mrs. Harris. Hinkler used the time to carry out checks on his engine, taking tappet clearances and making other final checks. His flight plan had a slight inbuilt dilemma: he was leaving England during the night so as to reach Athens before nightfall the next day, but as he was flying via the Alps he also hoped he would not reach the mountains too early. He mentioned the Alps problem and the possibility of landing at Brindisi in Italy in response to a remark from Mrs. Harris during the meal. Other than commenting that he thought his flight would take about six days, there had been no other discussion of it.

The evening wore on and it approached 9:00 P.M. It was time to make the final phone calls. The first was to Jack Savage at Colindale 6075. Hinkler had no need to use a notebook to find that number: he had just spent almost four months at Savage's Skywriting hangar at Hendon. That was where all the work had been done on the Puss Moth, preparing it for the flight to Australia. Savage's business affairs were in a bad way as the result of interference by the Air Ministry in mid-1931 in an important contract Savage was negotiating. Hinkler knew Savage would still be at the Hendon hangar waiting for his call. Over the years the two men had developed a firm friendship based on personal respect.

Harris arranged a bed for Hinkler in the sick bay. After a final call, to Glasgow Western 5560, Hinkler had a drink of stout from a bottle placed by his bed. He had earlier purchased six bottles, one of which was presented to Mrs. Harris: the other four Hinkler put away in his plane. When he retired he asked not to be awakened until 1:15 A.M.

At the appointed time he rose, washed, shaved, and dressed. Harris prepared a pot of tea and Hinkler drank a cupful, following it with a second. The two men then stowed the in-flight refreshments that had been prepared by Mrs. Harris earlier in the evening—one egg, two cheese, and three tongue sandwiches, three thermos flasks of unsugared black coffee; and one thermos flask of water—in the Puss Moth. The aircraft looked trim and ready. It was a high-wing monoplane painted silver with crimson touches. There had been mud splashes on the wing when Hinkler landed at Fairey's aerodrome but these had since been washed clean by one of the company's work hands. With everything in readiness Hinkler donned his flying clothes.

Jack Savage and Dopey Lingham were in a waiting room. They had arrived in response to the earlier phone call while Hinkler was still asleep. Hinkler now joined them. Initially the intended takeoff time had been 2:00 A.M. However, a mist that shrouded the airfield when Savage and Lingham arrived had temporarily slowed the tempo of preparation. They pushed the Puss Moth from the hangar onto the apron. One of the Fairey Company's staff, Clifton by name, moved to the propeller and Hinkler climbed into the cockpit. The two men called to each other in the rigid procedural sequence for starting the engine, then Clifton swung the prop, and the engine fired. After satisfying himself that all was in readiness in the cabin, Hinkler stepped down from the aircraft. Time to leave England and be on his way. The sky was clear and it was almost 2:30 A.M.

There then had followed Hinkler's last farewells and the forty-minute delay just as he was about to commence his takeoff run. When that final mist cleared, he could see the car lights illuminating the runway in the far distance. The whole of the aerodrome was open to view, and despite his heavy load of fuel, Hinkler had taken off in half the length of the runway. The long delay while his engine was consuming precious fuel virtually made certain that his first landing would be at Brindisi, at the heel of Italy, rather than at Athens. There was no longer any problem about reaching the Alps too early.

Hinkler crossed the Channel and flew over Le Bourget, the Paris airport. It was still dark and the Puss Moth carried no navigation lights, but the French authorities had granted a special dispensation for this flight. Southeast of Paris Hinkler passed over Sens and the Othe Forest on a line to Mâcon. He was over Sens at 5:25 A.M. with the Gipsy Major pushing the aircraft along at a speed that would have given great satisfaction, had they known about it, to the de Havilland Company, which manufactured the engine. A French forester on the ground heard the aircraft flying overhead and wondered what kind of venture would take an airman aloft so early in the day.

Bert Hinkler expected to be over Mâcon about 6:45 A.M. There

9

he changed course for Modane, reaching that town on time an hour later. He was now faced with the crossing of the Alps. His route took him over Colle di Moncenisio, and he accomplished the passage without any problems. Almost thirteen years had passed since Hinkler had first flown over the Alps. How different things were then. The aeroplane was a small Avro Baby biplane. It had a thirty-five-horsepower engine, which gave a speed little more than half that of the cruising speed of the Puss Moth monoplane he now flew. Back then, in 1920, he had been filled with the ambition of youth and hopeful of flying home to his mother in Australia to honour a long-standing promise: when he left home for England at the end of 1913 he had assured his parents he would come flying back to them as a "real dinkum" pilot. Leaking oil helped put paid to his ambitions in 1920. The Avro Baby was an open-cockpit plane and he had flown the Alpine regions with his mouth open so that the coldness of the air would soothe a raging toothache. In 1933 he had no toothache but perhaps just a little heartache and weariness from personal events that had overtaken him in recent years. The flight in 1920 gave him instant fame, and his name had been on and off the front pages of newspapers ever since. Almost certainly he would never fly over the Alps again.

Hinkler continued on course for Spezia in Italy and reached that city shortly after 10:00 A.M. Italian time. Since passing Mâcon in France he had flown almost a straight line. The next deviation would take place at Florence. Hinkler watched the countryside below. He felt reasonably familiar with this region. He had served in Italy in 1918 during the war and had returned there on at least two other occasions since then.

Soon the Arno River and the unmistakable outline of Florence appeared. He marked his log. Six hours and fifty-five minutes had passed since his aircraft left the ground at the Great West Aerodrome. To the Italian citizens of Florence below him, the time on this Saturday morning was 11:05 A.M.

Soon Hinkler would have to make the final decision between Brindisi and Athens. The engine had run superbly, but the odds heavily favoured Brindisi.

A decision of a different kind was about to be forced upon him.

## Hinkler's Flights Compared—1920 and 1933

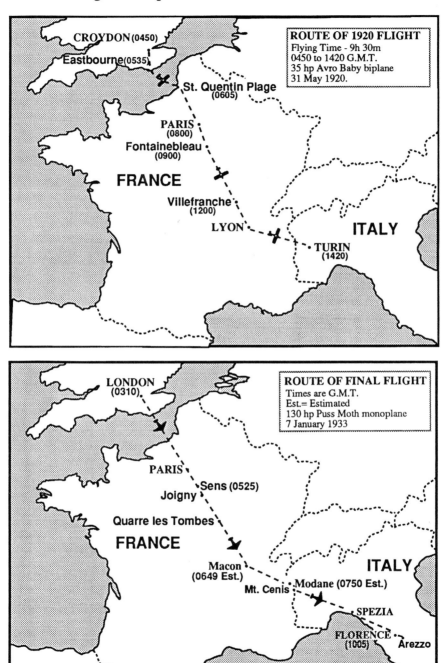

**ROUTE OF 1920 FLIGHT**
Flying Time - 9h 30m
0450 to 1420 G.M.T.
35 hp Avro Baby biplane
31 May 1920.

CROYDON (0450)
Eastbourne (0535)
St. Quentin Plage (0605)
PARIS (0800)
Fontainebleau (0900)
FRANCE
Villefranche (1200)
LYON
ITALY
TURIN (1420)

**ROUTE OF FINAL FLIGHT**
Times are G.M.T.
Est.= Estimated
130 hp Puss Moth monoplane
7 January 1933

LONDON (0310)
PARIS
Sens (0525)
Joigny
Quarre les Tombes
FRANCE
Macon (0649 Est.)
Mt. Cenis
Modane (0750 Est.)
ITALY
SPEZIA
FLORENCE (1005)
Arezzo
ROME

# PUSS MOTHS MUST BE MODIFIED

## Two Months to Alter all 'Planes in Use

(AUSTRALIAN CABLE SERVICE.)

LONDON, Thursday.—The Air Ministry has announced that certain specified modifications must be effected in Puss Moth cabin monoplanes within two months, otherwise their certificates of airworthiness are liable to be suspended or cancelled.

The de Havilland Aircraft Company informed a representative of The Daily Mail that the modifications will have to be carried out on Puss Moth machines in Australia. The necessary parts would be immediately forwarded to agents, and would be made available to all users of these machines.

THE Air Ministry's notice states that in the original type of Puss Moth failures have occurred in the curved V bracing tubes in the cabin roof at the front ends, near the weld to the front spar cross-tube.

The new regulation required that these members shall be examined for signs of cracking.

The notice also states that in isolated instances the diagonal members in the rear-most bay of the fuselage have been damaged by abnormal stresses from the tail-skid.

---

## "MYSTERY FLIGHT"

### HINKLER TO AUSTRALIA

(AUSTRALIAN CABLE SERVICE.)

LONDON, Monday.—It is reported that Mr. Bert Hinkler will shortly leave on a mystery flight to Australia. The de Havilland interests state he recently purchased a new, long-range engine, similar to Mrs J. A. Mollison's, for the Puss Moth, in which he flew by a circuitous route from New York to London.

He told a friend he would not waste time on the flight, when asked if he would attempt to break the record.

---

## HITCH IN PLANS

### HINKLER SECRETIVE

(AUSTRALIAN CABLE SERVICE.)

LONDON, Wednesday. — Although Squadron-Leader Bert Hinkler hopes to start for Australia before Christmas, a representative of The Daily Mail learns that the Air Ministry is not likely to grant a certificate of airworthiness to his machine. The certificate is necessary because he has had a new engine installed, but the aeroplane is registered in Canada, and the flyer wishes to retain the registration.

Squadron - Leader Hinkler desired to land at Wyndham, but he was informed by Australia House that this at present is not practicable. He refused to give any further details of his plans.

---

## PRESS REPORTS IN LATE 1932

*Reports having a bearing on the final flight as published by the Brisbane "Daily Mail". There was little left on which Hinkler could be said to be "secretive".*

### PUBLICATION DATES - 1932

| | |
|---|---|
| Top: | 18 November |
| Left: | 6 December |
| | 8 December |
| Below: | 13 December |
| Right: | 16 December |
| | 17 December |
| | 18 December |
| | 20 December |
| | 22 December |

---

## FLIGHT TO AUSTRALIA

### HINKLER LEAVES THIS WEEK

MELBOURNE, Monday.—It is not likely, as has been suggested in some quarters, that the flight of Bert Hinkler to Australia this week in a Puss Moth machine will be affected by the ban placed on these machines in Australia as a result of structural faults recently discovered.

It is stated in responsible circles that Hinkler's machine will have all the structural modifications to the tail and cabin ordered by the British Air Ministry recently, and that, as the machine had been passed as airworthy in England, it was not likely to be banned by the Australian authorities.

---

## PASSED FOR FLIGHT

### HINKLER'S MACHINE

(AUSTRALIAN CABLE SERVICE.)

LONDON, Thursday.—The Air Ministry has granted a certificate of airworthiness to Squadron-Leader Bert Hinkler's Puss Moth, despite the fact that its Canadian registration has been retained.

Squadron-Leader Hinkler has completed his plans, but declines to disclose the date of his departure for Australia. Officials say that unless he takes advantage of the present moon he may be obliged to postpone his departure for three weeks. His first stage probably will be Athens.

---

## IN FOUR HOPS

### HINKLER MAY COME

(AUSTRALIAN CABLE SERVICE.)

LONDON, Friday. — Though his plans are a close secret, it is believed that Squadron-Leader Bert Hinkler will attempt to reach Australia in four hops, the Evening News says. His machine is fitted with extra fuel tanks, enabling it to remain in the air for 25 hours.

Other fittings include ingenious inventions of his own, to facilitate long hops, including a new method of engine lubrication, and a specially-illuminated instrument board for night flying.

---

## HINKLER'S HOPES

### AUSTRALIAN FLIGHT

LONDON, Saturday. — The Daily Chronicle asserts that Squadron-Leader Bert Hinkler has stated that he proposes to start on his flight to Australia before Christmas. He believes that he can reach Darwin in four or five days.

---

## ATTEMPT LATER

### HINKLER AND RECORD

#### CIRCUS CONTRACT

(AUSTRALIAN CABLE SERVICE.)

LONDON, Monday. — Squadron-Leader Hinkler told the Australian Cable Service that he had postponed his flight to Australia.

He said that later he must go to Australia, for business reasons, and may attempt a record then. He confirmed the report that he had accepted a contract with a flying circus in the meanwhile.

---

## FLIGHT DELAYED

### CABLE TO MRS. HINKLER

AUCKLAND (N.Z.), Wednesday.—Mrs. Bert Hinkler, who arrived here on board the Rangitata from London, en route to Australia, received a cablegram at Auckland stating that her husband's departure on a flight to Australia had been delayed. Mrs. Hinkler will spend a short holiday in New Zealand before going to Australia.

# 2

# MISSING

Bert Hinkler was missing. No word reached London during the Saturday or Saturday night that he had landed at any of the airports around the Mediterranean. There were no reports that he had even been sighted anywhere along his anticipated route.

Most newspapers had some interest in the outcome of the flight. Hinkler was something of a national identity in Britain with a long series of aerial achievements behind him, achievements recognised by the award of the most prestigious medals and trophies. He had been a pilot in the British Schneider Trophy Team that competed in Baltimore, Maryland, in the U.S.A., in 1925. He was the recipient of three Britannia Challenge Trophies, the gold medal of the Federation Aeronautique Internationale, the gold medal of the Royal Aero Club, the Segrave Trophy, the Johnston Memorial Trophy for navigation excellence, and various others. He had received the Air Force Cross from the hands of the Prince of Wales. In 1922 he had been the first to fly an aircraft with an engine of one-thousand-horsepower and followed this the next year with a win in the light aeroplane trials at Lympne with a machine powered by the equivalent of a motorcycle engine. In 1924 he won the Grosvenor Cup. In 1928 he made the first solo flight from England to Australia, thereby emboldening many others to attempt the same feat, which they did in subsequent years. At the end of 1931 he completed a successful solo flight from New York to London by way of the Caribbean, South America, the South Atlantic, and northwest Africa in the same aircraft in which he was flying to Australia from the Great West Aerodrome: that 1931 flight had won for him the accolade from one knowledgeable critic of being "the leading pilot of the British Empire in the twelve years following the Armistice." In the Great

War of 1914–18 Hinkler had been decorated with the Distinguished Service Medal. For six years, 1921–26, he had been the chief test pilot for the Avro Company at its establishment at Hamble, near Southampton. Britain and Australia both claimed him as their own. This was the man who had now disappeared, apparently without a trace.

By Sunday morning a note of anxiety was evident in British newspaper reports. Both in England and on the Continent, government offices were closed over the weekend. The result was a frustrating silence. Reuters correspondents in France, Italy, and Greece confirmed there had been no sightings.

By the time the Monday morning press reached the streets the continuing silence had given rise to speculation of a different kind: was Hinkler in fact heading for Australia or was that just an assumption that everyone had made? The Air Ministry, under a bombardment of questions from the press, responded with a statement that it had no certain knowledge of Hinkler's route. If the Air Ministry's statement was correct, the airman's reputation was placed in serious jeopardy. Hinkler's night takeoff assumed a different significance. Some mystery, some secret, now seemed to underlie his flight, otherwise why would he have left England at night and not told anyone where he was going?

Confusion abounded. Where some commentators imputed secrecy concerning the route Hinkler intended to follow to Australia, others implied that the flight itself and its destination had been kept secret. The distinction between a "secret route" and a "secret flight" raised quite separate issues that had far-reaching implications. The confusion, however, could not have arisen had there been an organised body with knowledge of Hinkler's intentions. At first the press looked to the Air Ministry, but the ministry's response was negative. The press then sought information on Hinkler's petrol arrangements, only to be told by Shell Mex that the arrangements between the company and Hinkler were confidential, at the airman's request, and it was too early to release any details. This increased the mystery. What was it Hinkler was trying to hide? Why the secrecy?

Jack Savage was one of Hinkler's closest companions during the time that Hinkler spent preparing his Puss Moth for the flight at the Skywriting hangar at Hendon. Major Jack Savage, as he was known throughout England, had served in the Royal Naval Air Service in World War I and later organised the Savage Skywriting Company. This brought him world attention. His skywriters, all skilled airmen, had performed on a contract basis in about eighteen countries by 1933. On Sunday, immediately it was known Hinkler was overdue, Savage told a reporter what he knew of Hinkler's plans: Hinkler had intended to reach Athens in his first, long nonstop flight if he could, but if weather and fuel consumption told against him, he would land at Brindisi to refuel. There was no mystery about the flight. Hinkler's destination was his home country, Australia, and he was carrying messages to Savage's relatives there. Beyond that, Savage had no detailed knowledge of the flight. Other airmen spoke up with somewhat similar understandings of Hinkler's intentions, but like Savage, little notice was taken of them, mainly because of the position adopted by the Air Ministry.

If there were no organisations that could speak with authority on Hinkler's behalf, was there any individual or body of individuals who could provide acceptably authentic information? It was known that Nancy Hinkler was not in England and that the Hinkler home in Southampton was locked up and being looked after by a neighbour. Nancy had gone to New Zealand on the *Rangitata* in November 1932—somewhat prematurely in view of the delays that occurred after that time in Hinkler's plans—and she was staying at a hotel in Auckland. When contacted Nancy said she had received a cable from Bert some time before the takeoff but was not aware of his precise intentions at the time he left England because the delay had caused a change in his plans.

The British *Daily Herald* newspaper contacted the air ministries of France and Italy in the hope that, thus directly alerted, the air forces of those countries might keep a careful watch during their routine flying operations for the downed aircraft or for any evidence of wreckage. In continuing his search for information on the local London scene, the air correspondent of that newspaper made a surprising discovery. An aviation identity, Mr. Hazell Jones, whose name was similar to that of an official at the Air Ministry in London—they may have been one and the same person—reported that Hinkler had told him a woman was to be left in charge of his affairs. Should any difficulties be encountered during the flight she would be cabled, Hinkler said, but he had not mentioned her name at the time. The *Daily Herald* published this new twist in its edition of Tuesday, 10 January. Three days had passed since Hinkler left England. As far as the *Daily Herald* could discover, after considerable enquiries, no one had been left in charge of Hinkler's affairs. Other London newspapers were in much the same position.

That same afternoon Shell Mex ended the mystery. It released the route along which it had positioned stocks of petrol for Hinkler's aircraft. The procedure of laying down petrol was an essential precondition for any long-distance flight, and without it an airman could find himself stranded in a strange country. The route right through to Australia was Athens, Stamboul, Konya, Aleppo, Baghdad, Bushire, Jask, Karachi, Jhansi, Calcutta, Akyab, Rangoon, Victoria Point, Alor Setar, Singapore, Batavia, Surabaya, Bima, Koepang, and Darwin.

There was additional information that the petrol company had derived direct from Hinkler shortly before his departure. If conditions during the flight were satisfactory, he would cross the Alps. Otherwise he would fly a longer route down to Marseilles and then follow the coast route to avoid the high mountains. He might possibly stop at Brindisi to refuel.

Instead of silencing the commentators, this information seemed only to stimulate them further. It was now said that Hinkler had made a great fuss over a route that had proved to be only the ordinary route taken by aviators.

Hinkler's reputation would be left in tatters if the accusations were true, which of course they were not. Although the press and public did not become aware of it, the release of the route by Shell Mex was something of an embarrassment for the Air Ministry. Hinkler had provided the Ministry with exactly the same information. Now there was an attempt at further official concealment and self-justification: the Ministry said that Hinkler's route was still too uncertain for the Ministry to be able to ask particular countries to maintain a special watch for any wreckage or signs of the airman himself. The request would have to be more general. It asked the BBC to provide similar broadcasting organisations in a number of European countries with the information relating to Hinkler's disappearance and request them to broadcast it to their audiences. This action made it appear that some real problem existed with regard to the information supplied by Hinkler to the Air Ministry.

There was no such problem. Originally, when Hinkler intended a flight to Australia in October 1932 he approached the Ministry and provided an itinerary of his proposed flight. It was to have started on 14 October at Croydon and to have finished at Darwin on 29 October. The route was via Vienna and Sofia to Constantinople, thence by way of Konya and Aleppo to Baghdad and Bushire on the Persian Gulf. As the colder weather approached and Hinkler's departure was delayed, he felt it necessary to alter the route. It was then he advised the Air Ministry of his intention to fly through France and Italy to Athens and along the Balkan coast of the Mediterranean through to Syria. In calculating distances and times and fuel consumption it became apparent to Hinkler that a night takeoff from London would be necessary if he was to land during daylight hours at Athens. This implied also a crossing of France in the hours of darkness. His aircraft lacked navigation lights and such a flight across France required special approval. On Hinkler's fortieth birthday, 8 December 1932, he spent some time with the director of civil aviation at the Air Ministry, Lt. Col. F. C. Shelmerdine, discussing his projected flight to Australia and the need to obtain permission from the French authorities. Shelmerdine made an acid comment to the effect that Hinkler had, "as usual," left everything until the last minute. Nevertheless, the French promptly granted permission once the application was lodged.

Thirty days after this discussion, with its concrete outcome in the form of approval from the French, the Air Ministry told the press that nothing was known of Hinkler's route.

The week following the commencement of Hinkler's flight passed and still there was no trace of Hinkler or his machine. He had simply vanished. It seemed no longer possible to hold any hope for his survival. No voice had arisen from the tumult in England to still, with the voice of authority, the allegations that were injuring Hinkler's reputation and creating myths about his last flight that would echo down the years.

Hinkler's reputation had become the victim of an inexorable process. When Hinkler worked at the A. V. Roe & Company's experimental establishment at Hamble between 1919 and 1928 testing all varieties of aeroplanes and autogyros,* there had been a fairly considerable staff employed there. From among such a group there were always some who would know reasonably closely what Hinkler's intentions were or where answers could be found. The Avro establishment closed, and the staff distributed themselves throughout the aviation industry. It was no longer a relevant support group able to speak out on behalf of the missing airman. Hinkler was in Australia for much of 1928 and for two years after that he had been associated with a Southampton friend, Rowland Bound, in a joint venture to build the Ibis, an amphibian designed with Australian conditions in mind. Afterwards, between 1930 and 1932, Hinkler spent a lot of time in Canada and the U.S.A. Again he lacked a circle of close acquaintances who could have spoken up at a time of crisis, though he did spend a period at de Havilland in Canada and some of the staff there knew what he was planning. However, in January 1933, they were in Canada, and it was in England that the problem arose concerning Hinkler's flight plans. In any case the de Havilland information was likely to be outdated.

From September 1932 until 6 January 1933, Hinkler was working on his aircraft at Hendon Aerodrome in one of the hangars of the Savage Skywriting Company. Because of Savage's unfortunate business situation there were only two men at Hendon who might have learned Hinkler's intentions. One of them, Jack Savage, had spoken up immediately with accurate information, but he had been ignored. Apart from Skywriting, and given the singular circumstances in which Hinkler was placed, no other source of authoritative information existed.

Finally, Bert Hinkler was very much a "solo" flyer. His major feats were performed in light aeroplanes. He had no retinue and knew from bitter experience the impossibility of obtaining a sponsor. Sponsors wanted colourful personalities and "ballyhoo." Hinkler was an achiever not an actor. He stood little chance from the outset of obtaining a sponsor and, therefore, of leaving behind when he departed on the flight an authority who could speak on his behalf. The falsities and myths that emerged in the week following Hinkler's disappearance took on respectability with age and then were given the status of recorded history.

*For photograph of an autogyro see p. 182.

At week's end speculation centred on the possibility that Hinkler had been forced to descend in the water. The Channel, the Aegean Sea, and the Mediterranean were the three possibilities. If a vessel had picked him up it would by now have reported in, and in the absence of any such report it could only be assumed that no rescue had taken place. The remaining alternative was that Hinkler had come down in an inaccessible spot, been injured, and was awaiting rescue.

Hinkler's home at Thornhill was a short distance from the Southampton to Portsmouth Road. It was locked up. Bert was missing, with the increasing probability that he was dead, and Nancy was in New Zealand. The house and the household cat were being looked after by a neighbour.

On Sunday evening, 15 January, the house was broken into. A postman on his rounds discovered the break-in the next day and the Tuesday morning edition of the *Southampton Daily Echo* carried the full story. The postman, Fred Hailey, had called at the house on Monday morning at eight o'clock and found the dining room window broken. The police, with assistance from the neighbour who held the key, carried out an investigation. They found the interior of the house in total disorder. No attempt to conceal the intrusion had been made. Contents of drawers and cupboards were strewn over the floor. A photograph of Bert Hinkler's mother had been thrown on the floor and the face trodden in. The intruders—and it seemed generally to be assumed that there had been more than one—left the house through the back door, which opened into a conservatory. They then forced the lock on an adjoining shed. After a comprehensive inspection the police concluded that the only items that had been removed were four two-gallon tins of petrol taken from the shed.

The intruder, if there was but one, was clearly not a common thief. Under cover of darkness he or she had arrived and departed by car, and obviously was much in need of petrol for a long return journey: eight gallons would take most cars to London. Someone, who apparently had taken a severe dislike to Bert Hinkler's mother, had been searching for something that was desperately needed. The intrusion took place because it had been compelled by some necessity, but there was nothing to indicate the nature of that necessity.

19

# First Canadian Aircraft to Fly into Britain

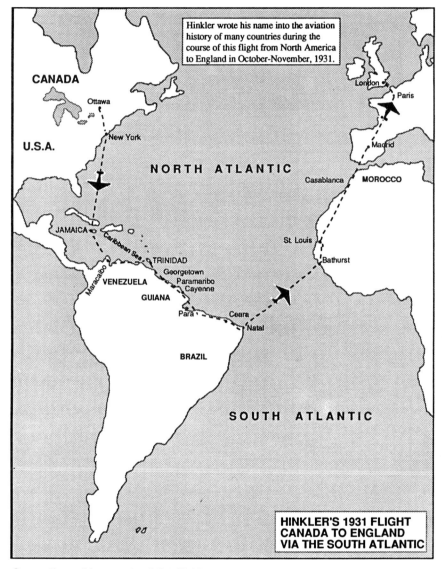

Hinkler wrote his name into the aviation history of many countries during the course of this flight from North America to England in October-November, 1931.

CANADA

Ottawa

U.S.A.

New York

NORTH ATLANTIC

London

Paris

Madrid

Casablanca    MOROCCO

JAMAICA

Caribbean Sea

TRINIDAD

Georgetown

Paramaribo

Cayenne

St. Louis

Bathurst

Maracaibo

VENEZUELA

GUIANA

Pará

Ceara

Natal

BRAZIL

SOUTH ATLANTIC

HINKLER'S 1931 FLIGHT
CANADA TO ENGLAND
VIA THE SOUTH ATLANTIC

**Some other achievements of the flight:**
• First aeroplane flight from New York to Jamaica
• First British aeroplane to cross the Caribbean Sea
• First aeroplane flight from Jamaica to Venezuela
• First solo flight across the South Atlantic ocean
• First successful flight from west to east across the South Atlantic

# The Hinkler Family, and Nancy

Frances and John Hinkler are seated with the youngest member of the family, known as Queenie, in front. Others, left to right, are George, Bert, May, and Jack.

*F. A. Palm*

Nancy, extreme right, played tennis with the Hamble Club. Her partner in mixed doubles was a Hamble draughtsman, Geoff Stride.     *Mrs. Ted Lawrence*

# 3

# Reaction in Bundaberg

Bert Hinkler was the eldest of the five children of John William and Frances Atkins Hinkler. He was born on 8 December 1892, at Bundaberg in Queensland. The youngest of the family, Frances Annie, was born on 8 December 1904, exactly twelve years later; in that period Frances Hinkler had given birth to two sons, Jack and George, and another daughter, who was known as May to the family though her given names were Beatrice Mary. The daughter Frances Annie was never called anything but Queenie.

Hinkler's father died in 1927, but in 1933 Frances Hinkler still lived in the house where her son Bert was born.

The last message to the Bundaberg home by Hinkler was a cable sent late on 7 December 1932, the day before his interview with Shelmerdine at the Air Ministry. Intended for Queenie it read:

> Many happy returns confidential coming home soon so please save my share cake love and kisses
>
> Bert

The *Bundaberg Daily News and Mail* published messages despatched from London by the Australian Cable Service, and the Hinkler family were able by this means to keep themselves informed on delays that occurred subsequent to the sending of the cable. When Hinkler failed to arrive for Christmas the family knew that he could not be much longer delayed.

The flight started at the Great West Aerodrome at 1:10 P.M. Saturday, Australian time. This left little margin for the news to reach reporting agencies in England and then be transmitted to Australia for the Sunday newspapers before they went to press the same evening. As a consequence no reference to the flight appeared in the Sunday newspapers circulating in Queensland at that time, the *Sunday Mail* and *Truth*. It was the radio that, on Sunday 8 January 1933, gave the family its first indication that Hinkler had taken off for Australia.

The Monday morning newspapers were able to report that no word of Hinkler's progress had come to hand from any of the towns on his route and that this was causing great concern. It was not a situation calling for family distress at so early a stage because it might be the result of a failure in the system of obtaining news from foreign countries. The headlines were disturbing, nevertheless, not only from what they suggested but from the fact that they were based on the position as it was understood to be at the end of thirty-six hours from the time the flight started. Frances Hinkler spent much time by the radio on Monday evening, hoping for some news and maintaining her confidence in her son's ability to get through.

By Tuesday morning the situation looked more ominous. Sixty hours after takeoff there was still no word in London. Hinkler had clearly suffered some misadventure in the early hours of the flight, and it was becoming a question of where that misadventure occurred and what its effect might be on Hinkler himself. Prominent airmen in England were confident of Hinkler's survival and this helped buoy the family's hopes.

On Wednesday Mrs. Frances Hinkler gave voice to a viewpoint that was gradually firming among members of the family. In a masterpiece of understatement the *Bundaberg Daily News and Mail* reported it this way:

> Mrs. Hinkler, who last evening displayed some concern about her son, is still hopeful that to-day will bring more reassuring news. Mrs. Hinkler informed us that while she has the fullest confidence in her son's ability to win through, she is not unmindful of the fact that it is possible for the machine to have been tampered with . . .

Not unmindful, indeed. The family had every reason to be well aware of that possibility because of an incident that had taken place at Coode Island in 1928 in which Jack Hinkler had been closely involved. Jack had discovered and thwarted an attempt on his brother's life. The perpetrator was never discovered. Now the circumstances of 1928 and of that attempt came to mind with renewed force.

The Bundaberg newspaper did not give the background to Frances Hinkler's observations. The casual reader could easily have gained the impression that the mother was defensively casting about to find reasons to explain away her son's lack of success on his current flight. But the facts of 1928 spoke for themselves.

This is the story of what occurred. Bert Hinkler had promised his parents when he left home for England in 1913 that he would return as a fully qualified pilot. He served through the whole of the war, first as a gunlayer with the Royal Naval Air Service and then finally as a fighter pilot with 28 Squadron, Royal Air Force. His first attempt to fly home, in a thirty-five-horsepower Avro Baby, ended in Italy in 1920. In April 1921 he arrived at his mother's gate in the same aeroplane, having shipped it to Sydney and flown to Bundaberg from there. That episode only partially satisfied Bert Hinkler's flying ambitions. He wanted to fly from England to Australia in his own aeroplane and then to find a flying job in Australia and remain there. In 1924 an opportunity came his way to acquire the Australian rights for Skywriting from Jack Savage, but Hinkler was unable to raise the necessary capital. The offer finally lapsed two years later with Hinkler still in England. Hinkler's idea had been to set up his own skywriting business in Australia. Savage Skywriters had won a big reputation and were well known in the United States as well as in Britain.

When Bert Hinkler in his own eighty-horsepower Avro Avian landed at Darwin on 22 February 1928, at the completion of the first ever solo flight from England, the whole of Australia rose to acclaim him. Britain acknowledged his achievement with the award of the Air Force Cross while the Australian government, which had recently been critical of local attempts at long flights involving sea crossings, granted him two thousand pounds and the honorary rank of squadron leader. Among the many hundreds of congratulatory messages that he received at that time was a telegram from his brother Jack, which said, "Congratulations thats the stuff to give em," and a cable from Jack Savage in England that suggested Hinkler might like to link up in Australia with a Skywriter named Lingham. Lingham had been sent out by Savage with the aim of selling the Australian rights to Savage's skywriting patents. Lingham arrived in Sydney by ship on 23 February, the day after Hinkler landed in Darwin. The presence of Lingham in Australia at that time was a coincidence of some magnitude; his visit lasted only a little longer than Hinkler's. There were actually two highly skilled flyers from England in Australia at the same time, but they received vastly disparate treatment from the newspapers and public.

As Hinkler toured Australia in 1928 to the acclaim of the multitudes wherever he went, acclaim backed in many cases by tributes in cash or other gifts, the years of adversity seemed behind him. In Melbourne, however, he earned the displeasure of one Australian-born airman: Lingham, no less. It arose out of Lingham's difficulties in selling the Australian rights to Skywriting. When Hinkler was negotiating with Savage in 1926 he received a much more favourable offer than Savage had now authorised Lingham to offer to any prospective client. Innocent of the implications Hinkler imparted the details of Savage's earlier offer to an affluent Australian helping him with local arrangements in Melbourne. Lingham, who was headquartered in the same city, viewed the same affluent Australian—he referred to him as a "rich squatter"—as a prospective purchaser and was not much pleased with what occurred. Hinkler's popularity and associated publicity were also coming at a time when Lingham stood very much more in need of publicity for practical commercial reasons. Despite the fact that Lingham was born in Melbourne, he had spent most of his life in England and was certainly not anxious to protract his stay in Australia. In fact he couldn't wait to get on board a ship back to England. Anything that seemed likely in any way to frustrate that objective incurred his displeasure. He was moved at one time to write to Savage that "the prevarication, delay & slowness of these swines out here is driving me potty. You can't imagine the thrill I shall have as and when I see the shores of Australia receding in the distance."

There was, moreover, more to Lingham's presence in Australia than business considerations. He was virtually a "remittance man" banished by Savage "to the colonies" because of Lingham's involvement in a domestic situation relating to Jack Savage's wife, Pauline. This Lingham confided to an Australian airman with whom he became friendly.

The incident that made an indelible impression on Jack Hinkler in 1928 occurred in Melbourne. His brother, who had just returned from a flight to Western Australia, was preparing for a flight to the island state of Tasmania across Bass Strait. His Avro Avian aircraft was housed at a private aerodrome at Coode Island owned by the Larkin Company. At Hinkler's request the company had prepared a smaller oil tank for his aircraft while he was absent in the West. The tank was supplied with a connection already attached and ready for direct installation in the aircraft. Jack Hinkler filled the tank with oil and connected it to the engine. He then decided to test to ensure that there was a flow of oil through the pipe. To his surprise no oil came through. He commented on this to his brother, but Bert's response was that the oil was probably cold—a reasonable enough response as it was the beginning of May and the cold weather had already arrived.

Jack Hinkler was puzzled, and it was not in his nature to leave the matter unresolved. He let the oil tank stand for a while then persevered. There was still no sign of oil coming through. He disconnected the tubing, put it to his lips, and attempted to blow through it. The passage was obviously obstructed and he called his brother over. With the aid of a stick they pushed out a ball of cotton waste that had been forced into the tube about halfway along its length. Had it not been discovered the engine, starved for oil, would have seized over Bass Strait, with almost certain death for the occupants of the aircraft.

Neither man had any idea who the perpetrator might have been. Bert Hinkler reported it to officials of the Larkin Company and having done so told his brother that nothing further should be said about it. It was the act of some unidentified individual, not the company, but it was the company that would suffer grievously for it if the incident received publicity.

The two airmen visitors to Australia, Bert Hinkler and Lingham, returned to England later in 1928, Hinkler leaving at the end of September and Lingham in December. Lingham was known to acquaintances as Algie during the visit but he was known everywhere else in the flying world as "Dopey," and he signed his correspondence with that soubriquet.

The attempt on Hinkler's life at Coode Island took place almost five years before he set off on his 1933 flight to Australia but it made a permanent mark on family thinking. The puzzle as to the perpetrator remained. To the world at large the 1928 attempt was simply an incident, but to the Hinkler family in Bundaberg it was an ever-present reality and an interpretative principle to be applied whenever and wherever suspicious circumstances attached themselves to anything to do with Bert's flying. It was a principle very much in the mind of Hinkler's mother, Frances, when she gave the interview that was reported in the Bundaberg newspaper on Thursday, 12 January 1933.

In 1933, during the first week that Hinkler was missing, no word reached Bundaberg of any searches being launched from Britain. Then came the distressing news that the home at Thornhill had been ransacked. The Bundaberg press covered the break-in in detail. It seemed that the intruders had been searching for papers or documents, and as the family saw it, those documents must have been the plans for the Ibis, the amphibian aircraft built by Bert Hinkler and his partner Rowland Bound in 1929 and 1930. This reason was actually suggested in the first instance by a British newspaper, the *Chronicle*, and was conveyed to Australia in the message that reported the break-in. The family could think of nothing else that could be of such interest or importance as to warrant breaking and entering the Thornhill house at such a time. Nancy Hinkler, in New Zealand, was reported to the same effect.

The Ibis, however, had not attracted commercial support in the aviation world in over three years, and the aircraft itself was in the shed on the Thornhill property and available for "inspection" without any need to enter the house. This hardly supported the theory that the plans had the value ascribed to them by Hinkler's relatives. Pride in Bert's achievements had tended to distort the family's understanding of the relative significance of the Ibis. As days passed and no one was apprehended, the puzzle of the break-in joined with the longer-standing Coode Island sabotage episode as a source of family irritation.

The newspapers, with absolutely no concrete reports coming in concerning Hinkler's whereabouts, had by now exhausted all forms of conjecture. There were some small items about an apparent search in Switzerland by a British airman, but the search, of limited duration, produced nothing. Frances Hinkler's thoughts began to turn to Nancy, who was in Auckland, and it appeared she might return direct to England because of the break-in.

Nancy left New Zealand on 20 January on the *Marama* for Sydney and then joined the *Ormiston* for Brisbane. Her ultimate destination was Bundaberg. She was responding to a message from Frances Hinkler who, with her son George, met the *Ormiston* when it docked in the Brisbane River on 26 January. On hand also to greet Nancy was Lores Bonney, a well-known airwoman, whose husband, Harry Bonney, was a cousin of Frances Hinkler. Lores had her own aircraft and Nancy flew with her to Bundaberg on 28 January. Three weeks had passed since Bert Hinkler took off from the Great West Aerodrome.

Both Nancy and Frances Hinkler maintained an outward face of calm confidence in Hinkler's ability despite the lengthening period since he had disappeared, and they bolstered each other's spirits. Nancy stayed some weeks in Bundaberg, hoping daily for good news, but it never came. In 1928, during a visit with Bert under happier circumstances, she had also become very friendly with another Bundaberg family named Gruter. When this family, now resident in Brisbane, asked Nancy to stay with them before she went back to England, she was happy to accept. The daughters of the Gruter household found her pleasant, bright, and friendly. They had grown to young womanhood since first meeting Nancy in 1928. They found her brave, too, for before the visit was over, Nancy suffered increasingly from bad dreams and nightmares.

She had a charm of voice and manner and a certain grace to her foot movements as she moved to a rhythm. But the children, being observant, sensed something more about this visitor from England, something that was like a tide about to break over the banks that contained it. Nancy had some secret sorrow, a sorrow that was somehow separate from, yet connected with, the tragedy of Bert Hinkler's as yet unexplained disappearance. It seemed to enshroud her, but it was never made tangible. The sorrow remained locked up.

Bundaberg was at a great distance from the centre of action. During the early months of Hinkler's disappearance, the difficulties of overseas communication and the lack of a central authority in possession of all the facts placed at a disadvantage those who were closest to Hinkler by family ties. They were unable to influence the course of events in England. Nor were they able, during those crucial early months, to obtain a clear picture of what was really going on.

# Hinkler at Coode Island—1928

Bert Hinkler in the workshop at Coode Island Aerodrome. There are inlet and outlet connections to the tank; Hinkler's finger is partly concealing one. Hinkler's brother recalled the dimension of the pipe on the oil tank as approximately one inch. This corresponds closely enough with the visible outlet. *T. F. Roberts*

Hinkler's Avro Avian at Coode Island, Melbourne, 1928. *T. F. Roberts*

## Puss Moth CF-APK

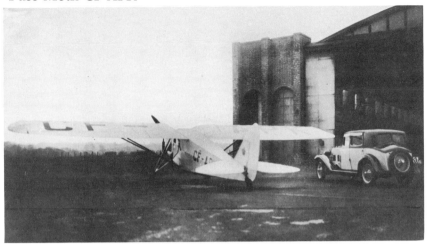

During Hinkler's absence in U.S.A. in 1932 the Puss Moth was hangared at South-ampton. He prepared the aircraft at Hendon Aerodrome, London, for his 1933 flight. His aircraft was the subject of an article in *Flight* on 15 December, 1932. In the days following Hinkler's disappearance it should not have been difficult to establish from witnesses, or *Flight* magazine staff, that the aircraft was coloured silver with crimson trim.

## Avro Baby G-EACQ

Hinkler's first major international non-stop flight took place in 1920. He flew the 35 hp Avro Baby (shown above at the 1919 Aerial Derby at Hendon) from England across France to Italy and descended at Turin because of an oil leak. On the flight he made his first aerial crossing of the Alps. The Avro Baby had a top speed of 80 mph. By contrast the 1933 Puss Moth had a *cruising* speed of 110 mph.

# 4

# SILVER AND YELLOW

Shell Mex released the full details of Hinkler's route in London on Tuesday afternoon, 10 January, thus opening the way for a possible search effort. Hinkler had not crashed in England and the possibilities of his having suffered some mishap commenced at the English coast where he began the crossing of the English Channel. The difficulty facing Bert Hinkler's friends, who were contemplating organising a search, was to try to find some means of limiting the area in which the search could take place. Normally when an aircraft disappeared on a long flight, there were reports of sightings, including some that were accurate and many that were imaginary or erroneous. But what was to be made of a situation where there were no reports at all? Hinkler may have been forced down in the Channel, in which case a search would be pointless after such a lapse of time, or he may have crashed into some obstruction lying in his path as he flew across France and Italy. The Alps on the border between France, Italy, and Switzerland seemed the most obvious area for any search to start.

No official action was taken to organise a search and an unofficial committee was formed by friends of Bert Hinkler. It was composed of Dr. S. Webb of the Empire Marketing Service; Mr. F. W. Strack, who reportedly had been "general manager of the Primary Producers, Bank of Australia"; Capt. T. H. Bailleau and Mr. A. N. Bishop. In a statement made on Saturday, 14 January, Bishop indicated that the committee had agreed to support a search of the Alps by a well-known airman, Capt. W. L. Hope. Contributors included Arthur E. Whitelaw, an Australian who was connected with the Preservine Soap Company. Some two hundred pounds was still required to help finance the search. Hope, who was the proprietor of an air taxi company, had offered earlier in the week to search the Alpine regions if others could fund a portion of the cost.

On Saturday, 14 January, Hope left the Stag Lane Aerodrome near London in his Hawk Moth but returned after a short flight because of heavy fog. He flew out successfully the following day. Accompanying him to Switzerland was a *Daily Mirror* photographer, W. G. Heanly. Stag Lane was the headquarters of the de Havilland company and a natural focus for aircraft produced by that company. Some confusion must have been caused by the number and variety of de Havilland aircraft that Hope had seen using the airfield for he had the impression Hinkler's Puss Moth was coloured yellow. There was little likelihood that Hinkler's Puss Moth, which was silver with some minor crimson trim, could be sighted against a background of snow, but the idea that it was yellow, however erroneous, was some encouragement to searchers.

Hope and Heanly were back in Paris on Saturday, 21 January. Their few days in Switzerland helped to keep hopes alive that Hinkler might be found but also caused great controversy. The highly coloured and inaccurate reports of their activity published in Britain roused the ire of Swiss authorities. Complaints were made at such a level that they were investigated behind the scenes in Britain. The findings, which were not complimentary of Hope's activity, were not publicised. Bert Hinkler, probably most of all, would have recognised the hopelessness of locating a small wrecked aircraft in the vastness and depth of the Alpine snows and understood Hope's lack of search commitment. On the credit side Hope's presence was the cause of a flurry of search activity by the Swiss themselves. With the withdrawal of Hope's Hawk Moth from Switzerland, any prospect of finding Hinkler alive was at an end.

The British flyers passed through France quickly on the return to England. For one Frenchman this was a reason for dissatisfaction. M. P. Saby, an inspector of forests and waterways at Sens, southeast of Paris, had hoped that some use might have been made of their aircraft to have a comparatively small area, the Othe Forest, searched from the air. It is possible the British flyers had no knowledge of Saby's need for assistance, but in any case there were a number of witnesses in Switzerland who claimed to have seen an aircraft similar to Hinkler's flying through mountainous regions on Saturday, 7 January, and it seemed unlikely Hinkler could have crashed in the region south of Paris referred to by Saby.

That Hinkler had no reason to fly over Switzerland, which was far to the north of any route he might have taken on his way through France and Italy, seemed not to be a factor taken into account in assessing the relevance of the various reports.

Saby was the man who heard an aircraft fly over Sens in the dark at 5:25 A.M. on the morning Hinkler left England. When Saby learned from the French press that the British airman Hinkler was missing on a flight to Australia, he reported his information to the Le Bourget Airport authorities. His "sighting" met every test of arithmetic and logic. Sens was on a quite likely route and the time of 5:25 A.M. dovetailed precisely with Hinkler's departure time from London and the speed of his Puss Moth aircraft.

The Air Ministry was advised from Paris of Saby's report, a fact of which Saby became aware when the *Daily Mail* telephoned on Tuesday, 17 January. The newspaper informed him that no sightings from any other place had been reported to the Air Ministry; then in its issue of the following day, the *Daily Mail* announced that this was the first clue to Hinkler's disappearance received by the Ministry. In France that same Wednesday morning, spurred by the British interest, Saby set off early to discover whether others living in his region had heard or seen the aircraft.

According to reports in the British press over the weekend of 21 to 22 January, a preliminary search of the Othe Forest was unsuccessful. In Australia a government-controlled radio station broadcast an unconfirmed report that Hinkler's body had been found in the Alps. This was soon withdrawn, but not before it had caused distress to anxious relatives of the airman. These reports coincided with the arrival back in England of the search team from Switzerland. Fourteen days had passed since Hinkler disappeared and winter weather had settled over Europe. It was no longer possible to hope for Hinkler's survival. With the funds it still possessed, the London Search Committee resolved to create a memorial to Hinkler and scheduled a memorial service for 5 February at the City Temple. Almost instantaneously a strange rumour arose, perhaps generated by the finality implied by the memorial service, that Hinkler had been found alive in a hut in the Alps. The rumour spread widely and quickly, even reaching Australia.

Interference with the search committee's plans came at once and from an unexpected quarter. To this time the members of the committee had assumed, quite reasonably, that anyone with Hinkler's interests at heart, or who possessed any relevant information, would long since have contacted them. Now they discovered the existence of a solicitor claiming to represent Hinkler's interests. Without ceremony the solicitor—who seemed at this time to have experienced no difficulty contacting the committee, whatever the reason might have been for his previous lack of contact—instructed them that the service be cancelled forthwith. The committee's actions had originated from a genuine concern for Bert Hinkler at a time when officialdom remained inactive. It possessed the moral authority to organise the memorial service for there had been no evidence of any interest by others in the missing airman, either official or unofficial. When challenged, however, the committee was vulnerable because it lacked both legal and official standing.

The solicitor, L. V. Pearkes, certainly did not mince words: "I gave Mr. Bishop instructions to cancel it before I heard anything about the rumour," the *Daily Herald* of 31 January 1933 quoted him as saying. The solicitor went on: "Acting on the instructions of a relative of Hinkler, I took steps to see that the service was not held." The identity of the relative who gave this instruction to the solicitor was somewhat obscure. Readers of the *Daily Herald* would not have been aware of it, but all the known relatives of Bert Hinkler were in Bundaberg, where Nancy had just arrived after being on the move since leaving New Zealand on 20 January. The solicitor himself was unknown in Bundaberg.

Saby, in France, renewed his enquiries after the stimulus of the *Daily Mail* call of 17 January, but the results were unknown in England, though the search of the Othe Forest, which was reported, was based on Saby's information. Saby had set off on the morning of Wednesday, 18 January, to glean what further information might be available from others on the flight path of the aircraft. He established that the aircraft was heard over at least four separate places, including a woodcutter's hut in the forest. The following morning Saby learned that the passage of the aircraft had been noted at six more villages. With time pressing, he asked the Chief of Police at Yonne to make some enquiries for him. From this source he learned on Friday evening that the aircraft had passed over two further places, Avalon and Quarre-les-Tombes. All the localities were in a straight line, and marking them on a map, Saby reached the conclusion that Hinkler was crossing France from the Channel on a line generally directed towards Nice on the Mediterranean coast. The line passed close to Mâcon.

Saby prepared a long report in his own language, which was forwarded through the British air attaché in Paris at the end of January to the director of civil aviation in Britain. Because of the lapse of time since Hinkler disappeared and the onset of winter weather over Europe, there was no longer any question of making a search to succour the missing airman. All that remained was to locate the wreckage and establish the how and why of the event. At this time the aviation magazines *Flight* and *Aeroplane* published lengthy memorial tributes to Hinkler.

Nevertheless, the interest of solicitor Pearkes seemed reinvigorated by Saby's detailed report and he and the secretary of the Royal Aero Club called upon the French air attaché in London. The solicitor's attitude towards finding what could now only be wreckage and a body contrasted rather sharply with his inertia during the period when a successful search might have assisted the injured aviator.

# HUNTING FOR PLANE THAT MAY BE HINKLER'S

A CAREFUL search is to be made to-day in the Forest of Othe, about 80 miles to the south-east of Paris, following a report last night that the wreckage of an aeroplane —which may have been Squadron-Leader Bert Hinkler's—had been seen there.

Hinkler left London on the morning of January 7.

At 5.30 on the same day the machine was seen flying over Dixmont in the Yonne. then some minutes later at Bussy-en-Othe.

The machine has not been reported at any other place since.

Yesterday the President of the Aero Club of the Yonne flew with his machine over a great part of the forest, but visibility was bad and his exploration yielded no result.

### NIGHT MESSAGE

Other airmen will fly over the forest to-day (says Reuter).

Speaking on the long-distance telephone to London. the officer in charge of the Gendarmerie at Auxerre said:

"We learned during the night of a report that an aeroplane had fallen in the Forest of Othe, near Bussy-en-Othe

"The aeroplane is reported to have been seen earlier at Sens by the side of the forest"

The forest is in the line Hinkler would probably take on his proposed hop from England to Brindisi.

Capt W. L Hope is still searching over the Alps for signs of the lost airman, but so far he has met with no success.

---

## REPORTED TRACES OF MR. HINKLER

### SEARCH IN BERNESE OBERLAND

FROM OUR CORRESPONDENT

GENEVA, Jan. 17

Captain Hope, who has now moved his headquarters from Basle to Lausanne, yesterday concluded his aerial search for Mr. Hinkler over the Jura range, though

---

# A FOILED HOPE

## Hinkler's Plan Divulged

### USUAL ROUTE

("Sun" Special)
LONDON, Tuesday.

FEELING bound to break a pledge of secrecy in the circumstances, the Shell-Mex Company reveals to "The Sun" that Bert Hinkler intended to follow the usual route in the early stages of his flight to Australia.

The company, becoming anxious for the airman's safety, states that Hinkler told them in confidence that he would go via Bagdad and Karachi, his first stop being Brindisi or Athens, according to the weather.

The company discounts the theory that Hinkler may have followed another route of his own devising.

---

# Mrs. Hinkler's Anxiety

AUCKLAND, Monday.

Mrs. Hinkler, wife of the airman, who has not been reported since he left London for Australia, early on Saturday, is in Auckland.

She is anxiously waiting for news of her husband, and is prostrated by the suspense.

Mrs. Hinkler left England by the Rangitata. and reached Auckland on December 21 last.

She said that she was on her way to Sydney, but word from her husband advised her to wait in New Zealand until she heard from him again.

---

Top left: Daily Herald (U.K.) 19.1.33
Left: Times (U.K.) 18.1.33
Top Right: Sydney Sun 12.1.33
Above: Sydney Sun 9.1.33

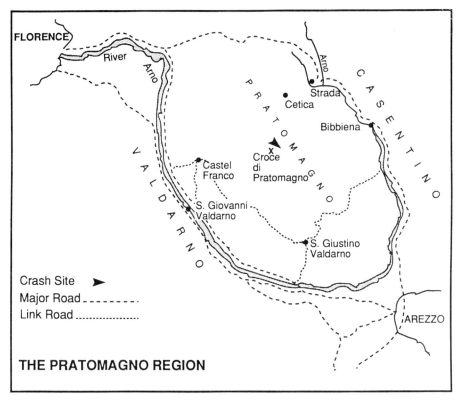

## THE PRATOMAGNO REGION

FLORENCE

River

Arno

P R A T O M A G N O

Strada

Cetica

Bibbiena

CASENTINO

Croce
di
Pratomagno

Castel
Franco

VALDARNO

S. Giovanni
Valdarno

S. Giustino
Valdarno

AREZZO

Crash Site ➤
Major Road _ _ _ _ _ _ _ _ .
Link Road ...................

Map of the Pratomagno region showing how the crash occurred about mid-way between Florence and Arezzo.

A view across Arezzo to the mountains of Tuscany.

# 5

# APRIL 1933

The interest of the British as expressed to the French air attaché persuaded Saby to extend his enquiries from Sens across France to Switzerland. Saby had not actually seen the aircraft that passed over Sens in the early morning hours, so the only visual impression of Hinkler's aircraft was provided by others. It was unfortunate that Saby's advisors were ill-informed on the same subject. His enquiries traced the route taken by a red aircraft on the day Hinkler disappeared.

Hinkler had flown across France on a straight line until he reached Mâcon on the Saône River north of Lyons, then he altered course for Modane, which is to the east of Grenoble. This route was far to the south of Switzerland.

The erroneous information supplied to Saby caused him to pick up the trail of a red aircraft which, at Morvan, apparently crossed the route flown by Hinkler and flew eastwards. He tracked this aircraft from the Morvan to Louhans, well to the north of Mâcon in France, and then to Switzerland. He summarised the result of his enquiries in a report sent to the British Embassy in Paris on 21 April. From the movement of the aircraft in Switzerland, Saby drew the conclusion that it would probably be found in Piedmont in Italy, where a violent snowstorm was said to have occurred on the day of Hinkler's disappearance. Pearkes, the solicitor who'd stopped the memorial service at the end of January, had followed Saby's enquiries keenly and knew the result before the report was finalised. On the same day that Saby completed the summary of his search efforts, 21 April, Pearkes enquired from Shelmerdine, the director of civil aviation, as to whether there were any official reports from Italy or Switzerland that could be used to reinforce the main thrust of Saby's report. His reason was clearly stated:

> Having regard to the information I have already obtained I propose to make an early Application to the Court to presume death and any information you could give me regarding Official Reports would be of material assistance.

At the same time he offered a criticism of the Hope search, which, all things considered, was rather peculiar:

> I have ascertained that the Swiss authorities carried out an exhaustive search which was hampered rather than assisted by the unofficial visit there of Hope. I gather that he informed the Authorities that the machine was painted yellow when everyone else said it was red with the result that any reports which arrived about a red machine were disregarded. . . .

With this criticism of Hope, Pearkes made several things clear without intending to: his attitude towards the now-disbanded search committee (as implied by the linking of the words *hampered* and *unofficial*) and his own inability to state the correct colour of Hinkler's aircraft, which reflected a further lack of awareness as to where to obtain correct information. Furthermore, it was Hope's visit that stimulated the Swiss search, a fact which must be taken into account in any criticism of the British airman.

While Pearkes waited for a reply, a woman's hands placed a wreath at the Cenotaph in Melbourne, Australia. It was 25 April, Anzac Day, the day each year on which Australia commemorated those who had served in the war of 1914–18. The hands were Nancy's and the name on her wreath was that of Squadron Leader Bert Hinkler, AFC, DSM, who had served his country from September 1914 until the end of the war, making more than 120 operational flights in the process. Soon afterwards Nancy boarded the RMS *Strathaird* for the passage back to England.

Shelmerdine had not received any official reports from the countries mentioned by Pearkes, and he responded immediately to that effect in a letter that Pearkes could not have received prior to 26 April. Events concerning Hinkler's disappearance, however, were now moving to their climax and in such a manner as would give momentum to an entirely new sequence of events.

When Hinkler arrived over Florence on 7 January at 11:05 A.M., he set a new and more southerly course to follow the valley of the Arno. He intended to keep the mountains on his left until he reached a point about eighty miles (128 km) south of Florence. On reaching that point he would make an easterly turn, cross the Apennines, and head for Brindisi. Since takeoff things had gone well. Unknown to Hinkler, as the seconds sped away, that situation was about to change—abruptly and violently.

In the region through which Hinkler was flying, the southerly side of the Apennines—called the Valdarno side—rose to his left. Where the northern slopes descended on the farther side, the region was called Casentino. About a week after Hinkler's flight, the snow fell and the winter became bitterly severe. Throughout the length of the Apennines, the snow covered everything.

On Thursday, 27 April, while Pearkes was contemplating Shelmerdine's response, Gino Tocchioni, a twenty-five-year-old carbon collector, left his home at Castelfranco di Sopra on the Valdarno side of the mountains and climbed towards the highest point in that region, Pratomagno. He crossed the spine of the mountain about eighty metres below the summit and began a descent on the Casentino side. It was nearly 10:00 A.M. On the heights the snow was still more than a metre deep. The cold was penetrating, but the slopes of the mountain were almost clear of snow. Tocchioni was working his way down a spur between the summit and Poggio del Lupo, the Hill of the Wolf, when his eye caught a flash of white some distance from him and higher up. Curious and surprised, he climbed to the site. With still some distance to go, he realised he had stumbled on a tragedy. It was the wreckage of an aircraft. Tocchioni looked about him. Where was the pilot? Farther up the mountainside he found a wing beside a tree with its top broken, various items which appeared to have fallen from the aircraft, and a large suitcase. Some distance along the mountainside from the main wreckage, at a place known to the locals as the Prato alle Vacche, he discovered a body lying on its back. Tocchioni was struck immediately by the posture of the body. It was that of a man who had composed himself as though for sleep. The facial area was disfigured by the attack of a wild animal, and it seemed the same animal, probably a wolf, had attacked the airman's left wrist also. The airman's watch and bones from the wrist were in their place beside the body. From all appearances the body was well preserved, a result of the prolonged winter.

The scene filled Tocchioni with a mixture of emotions—surprise, excitement, and trepidation. It was obvious that the *carabinieri* should be notified and at once. He began his return to Castelfranco, but after going only a short distance, he encountered another carbon collector, Raffaello Cari. Together they returned and examined the wreckage and body. Time wore on. Finally they climbed the mountainside, crossed the spine, and began the descent of the Valdarno slope. At Castelfranco they reported their discoveries to the *carabinieri*. There was to be further delay because the Casentino side of the mountains, where the wreckage lay, was under the jurisdiction of the *carabinieri* headquarters at Bibbiena on the other side of the mountains. A message reporting the discovery of a wrecked aircraft on the slopes below Pratomagno was transmitted to Bibbiena. A phonogram then relayed this message at 5:45 P.M. from Bibbiena to the *carabinieri* station at Strada-in-Casentino. The two carbon collectors had been instructed to make their way to Cetica, halfway down the Casentino side of the mountain, and wait there for the official party, which they were then to guide up to the crash site. It seemed Tocchioni and Cari, who had experienced a long day, were now about to experience a much longer night.

Under the mistaken impression, however, that the guides were to present themselves at Strada-in-Casentino, Marshal Romeo Aureli and *carabiniere* Giovanni Polini waited at Strada until a late hour. They then left for the mountain in the company of forestry officer Adamo Gambineri and his subordinate Loris Bruni. The group reached Cetica at midnight. During the night a second group from Strada joined them. They waited for daybreak before continuing the ascent to Pratomagno. The second group included a pharmaceutical chemist, Giuseppe Ghedini; a photographer, Donatello Cosci; and a reporter who appeared to be the local correspondent for *La Nazione*, a newspaper published in Florence. A light, presumably a campfire, could be seen burning on Pratomagno. No contact was made at Cetica with Tocchioni and

Cari, who almost certainly by now were asleep and quite unaware of the presence of the others.

The combined Strada groups set off early and began the three-hour climb. At 7:30 A.M. when nearing the top of the mountain spine below Pratomagno, a handkerchief being waved about in the distance attracted them to the correct site. They found the aircraft lying among bushes in what was virtually a small, cleared area surrounded by trees. Photographer Cosci began taking photographs from many angles.

Documents on the body quickly established the pilot's identity. A Canadian passport named the unfortunate airman as Herbert——who was born in Bundaberg, Queensland, Australia, on 8 December 1892. The surname, which was illegible, was said to have been effaced by the weather. Giuseppe Ghedini from Strada-in-Casentino, a chemist in private life, was also an officer in the Air Force Reserve, and from the documents and his observations he was soon able to say that Hinkler's aircraft was a Puss Moth bearing the Canadian registration markings CF-APK and that Hinkler had been engaged on a flight from England to Australia early in January when he met disaster on Pratomagno.

By now many hardy mountain men from the region were on the scene. Tocchioni and Cari, having missed the official party during the night, arrived from Cetica, but after two days on the mountain their roles were at an end. The *carabinieri* placed a guard on the wreckage and body immediately and began investigations. The aircraft lay stretched out from tail to engine in about its own length. The left wing and items from the baggage compartment, which had been found close together farther up the hillside, were listed and placed with the main body of wreckage. A petrol tank was found down the mountain past the body. The body itself was examined where it lay by Dr. Vettori. It could not be moved in any way until official approval was received. Theories as to how the aircraft came to be where it was began to develop.

The crash site was altogether singular, with a wall of mountain rising beside it and another wall rising a short distance in front. The wreckage was pocketed, well down the mountainside, and lying among bushes in what was virtually a small cleared area surrounded by trees. To the *carabinieri* the facts seemed to explain themselves. Hinkler had been crossing above the mountain when a wing came off his machine, and the rest of the aircraft then fell vertically into its final position. This tended to ignore some very salient features, which Ghedini commented on and which many of those early on the scene had already observed. The wing had been knocked off the aircraft when it struck a tree halfway down the mountain. The aircraft, "thus mutilated," then fell down the mountain onto the spot where it was found. The weakness in Ghedini's account seemed to be that it left unanswered the vital question: How did it come about that an airman of Hinkler's experience could get himself into such a position as to hit a tree so far down the mountain? Moreover, from the disposition of wreckage it was clear that the aircraft had come from the Valdarno side, yet the wreckage itself was on the Casentino side, and it was also quite apparent that the main body of the aircraft had fallen into its final position.

On one aspect of Tocchioni's discoveries there was no room for argument. *Carabinieri* headquarters at Bibbiena received the news from the Pratomagno contingent concerning the identity of the airman at 3:15 P.M. on Friday, 28 April. It notified the appropriate authorities, and that evening the British Embassy in Rome was informed. At the same time the first messages were reaching London. The further unusual sequence of events was about to unfold.

At midday on Saturday, 29 April, orders were received for the removal of Hinkler's body from the mountain. The *carabinieri* had been assisted by men from the mountain villages and these now took in hand the task of preparing the body. A zinc case was ready, and Hinkler's body, in a sheet, was placed inside and the case sealed. It was carried to the foot of the mountain in stages. A donkey was pressed into service to carry the zinc case down the steep mountain track as far as Cetica. A narrow winding road led down the mountain from Cetica and permitted car transport. At Pagliericcio, near the end of the descent, the body was placed in a walnut coffin prepared by a local carpenter, Lamberto Broggi. The transfer being completed, the car carrying the coffin continued to its destination, Strada-in-Casentino. There, at 8:30 P.M., the coffin was placed in the Casa del Fascia, the House of the Fascists. It was the night of 29 April. Candles burned beside the body throughout the night, and a guard of honour maintained a vigil.

The last day of April dawned. The women of Strada were busy with needles and cotton and cloth. There was no Union Jack available locally and they busied themselves making one. Local bandsmen practised the British national anthem and "Rule Britannia." At 6:00 P.M. the coffin, on the shoulders of members of the Regia Aeronautica, was carried through the streets in the presence of a vast assemblage of the citizenry. The burial was to take place at Florence. With due ceremony the coffin, draped with the British flag, was solemnly handed to the care of the officials from Florence and placed on the vehicle that was to carry it. A representative of the British Embassy was present. With him was Captain Cottarelli, whose responsibility it would now be to oversee all arrangements until the coffin was interred in the soil of Italy. As the cortege carrying the body made its way to Florence, heavy rain fell throughout the journey.

At the gates of Florence a guard of honour waited in the rain. A company of Black Shirts formed in procession and accompanied the coffin until it was laid in the place readied for it in the rooms of the Aero Club of Florence. It was 10:30 P.M. As the last minutes of April ticked away, a tripartite guard was mounted: *carabinieri* in full dress uniform, Black Shirts, and the Air Force Reserve officers of the Aero Club.

## Arezzo Organisations

Arezzo is a major city south-east of Pratomagno. Two Arezzo organisations—the Aero Club and the Ente Provinciale per il Turismo (the latter under the directorships of Dr. A. M. Droandi and Cmdre. Alessandro Mellini)—have played major roles in keeping the name of Bert Hinkler alive.

*E.P.T.*

Alessandro Mellini in his office at the Ente Provinciale per il Turismo, Arezzo. In 1975 he arranged for two Australians to use an alpine hut while they searched the Pratomagno mountains for the propeller blade lost in midair by Hinkler and took a keen interest in all developments. *Tom Wixted*

*Arezzo Aero Club*

Luciano Centini garbed for his role as a marshal for the annual Arezzo pageant, the Joust with the Saracen. A leading member of the Arezzo Aero Club, he flew many times over Pratomagno attempting to assess Hinkler's line of flight before the crash. Both Luciano and the Club were prominent during the 1974 investigations and the fiftieth-anniversary ceremonies in 1983. *Tom Wixted*

The body at Strada-in-Casentino

The Funeral in Florence

# 6

# MUSSOLINI

The identity and standing of Bert Hinkler had been established quickly and the implications were just as quickly evident to Il Duce, Benito Mussolini, when he heard of the discoveries made on Pratomagno. Among Hinkler's achievements was a flight across the South Atlantic, which had been performed solo and in a light aeroplane. Had Hinkler never achieved anything else this flight, in the circumstances of the time, stamped him as a hero. For such a man Italy must offer no less than a state funeral. Instructions were given accordingly. At the same time, 29 April, an official enquiry began taking evidence in the *carabinieri* barracks at Strada-in-Casentino. Witnesses were interrogated to establish the cause and manner of Hinkler's death, as required under Italian law. The document of most importance in identifying Hinkler—despite the effaced surname—was his Canadian passport, and the official Italian announcement of the state funeral was made in conjunction with the handing over of the passport to the British Embassy. The detail of the passport was given: It had been issued at Ottawa, Canada, on 18 March 1932.

Mussolini's decision created a stage upon which all the leading players in the Hinkler drama were about to soliloquise, or dramatise, their secret thoughts and attitudes on the death of a hero. Not all the main characters became clearly visible to the public. There were some who played out roles thousands of miles from Italy, and others who hid at times behind subterfuge. This is why, in 1933, some of the central characters were detectable only as silhouettes or shadows or even less. But because of Mussolini's action, all of them had to make their attitudes explicit.

London newspapers published their first reports of the sudden turn events had taken in Italy, though often without regard for accuracy, on Saturday, 29 April. The news reached Nancy on the same date as she travelled by the *Strathaird* to Fremantle, the last port of call in Australia. It came in the form of a radio message from a Western Australian newspaper. Nancy was having tea in the lounge with other passengers when the message was handed to her. Totally unprepared she dropped her cup and fled, seeking solitude to put her thoughts in order. News reports that had been received earlier by the ship's radio room and then suppressed were later made available to her in a censored form. The published details of injuries to Hinkler's body were horrific, and the descriptions of the crash scene were exaggerated and misrepresented the nature of the crash, so it was an act of consideration by the radio operators to withhold the more gruesome details.

Frances Hinkler, who was journeying across the continent by train to make her final farewell to Nancy at Fremantle, heard the news the same day when her train stopped at Cook near the South Australia–Western Australia border. A telegram from her son George was handed to her, and it broke the news of the finding of Hinkler's body. By coincidence, the small town of Cook had featured prominently in Bert Hinkler's flying achievements during his 1928 visit to Australia because he had landed there on his way to Perth after a record nonstop flight from Melbourne.*

When, on the same day, Bundaberg learned of Hinkler's death, public buildings flew their flags at half-mast.

In Australia the discovery of Hinkler's body and the wreckage of his aircraft was reported by Saturday afternoon newspapers, where such existed and then in the Sunday morning press. The news was mainly a summary of British press coverage received through agencies in London.

By an unusual coincidence the Hinkler Handicap, a race named in honour of Bert Hinkler after his 1928 flight to Australia, was being held at Eagle Farm Racecourse in the Queensland capital, Brisbane, that same Saturday afternoon. Hinkler had landed

---

*Cook also received a mention in Italy that same day when the Florence newspaper *La Nazione*, in its report of the discoveries on Pratomagno, referred to Hinkler's Melbourne-Cook record of 1928: "*Nel marzo 1928 Hinkler volo, senza scala, da Melbourne a Cook, un volo di mille miglia, e un 'record' di distanza per l'Australia.*"

on the racecourse when he visited Brisbane in March 1928, thereby avoiding the boggy conditions at the nearby aerodrome. The three place-getters in the Hinkler Handicap were Will Yet, ridden by B. Hornery; Hourly, ridden by F. Shean; and Ripolot, ridden by W. Vowles. Neither among the placed horses nor among those that were unsuccessful was there anything to provide an omen to reinforce the coincidence.* As a mark of respect to the airman whose body still lay at that time upon the place where it was found on Pratomagno, all the jockeys wore black crepe arm bands.

George Hinkler, in Sydney on a visit when he sent the telegram, expressed the family's wishes in a Brisbane newspaper interview:

> Could Bert express a wish it would be that he be laid to rest in his native Bundaberg. Although he roamed the world and his life was full of adventure in other lands, Bert at heart remained a home man. He said to me when last he visited the family at Bundaberg, "I would like to end my days in Australia." His letters to mother were couched in a similar strain, and I know that he would have stayed here after his flight from England in 1928 had there been anything doing, but circumstances denied him that wish. Our family desire that his body be brought back and buried in Bundaberg alongside the bodies of his father and grandfather. I cannot speak for Bert's widow but I believe she too would feel that he belonged to Australia. I am definitely sure that mother and my brother and sisters would be grateful if the Commonwealth Government gratified our wish, subject of course to the proposal meeting with the approval of Bert's widow.
>
> Until the actual news of his death came to hand, we all were optimistic, with the probable exception of mother. Bert had come through so often that, despite natural concern at his being missing so long, we believed that he would turn up, smiling, in the long run.
>
> But mother was different this time. Previously she never worried greatly. Now she had a feeling that something had gone wrong. We tried to restore her old confidence, but to no avail.
>
> Bert was always his mother's boy. Despite his crowded life of adventure, he always found time regularly to write to her. He was

*But a matter of inner significance, the question of Hinkler's will, was yet to be determined.

very happily married, too. In spite of the stern sphere in which his life was cast, Bert remained a sentimentalist. For that and other reasons I would like to see him brought home.

The Australian government was as quick as Mussolini to realise the national implications of the discovery of Hinkler's body. On the evening of Sunday, 30 April, the Australian prime minister, J. A. Lyons, announced that the Commonwealth government would make all necessary arrangements for the transport of Hinkler's remains to Australia for burial in his home state of Queensland. The government was waiting for the *Strathaird* to dock at Fremantle in order to ascertain the wishes of Nancy Hinkler, the airman's widow.

On Monday, 1 May, the Australian prime minister learned that it was Nancy's wish that Bert Hinkler's body should be returned to Australia. He announced immediately that all expenses would be met by the Commonwealth government and that a state funeral would be held in Brisbane with full honours. The Queensland premier, W. Forgan Smith, concurred at once with the statement by the prime minister. The Australian government's resident minister in London, S. M. Bruce—a former prime minister himself—immediately cabled Australia for instructions.

The body of Bert Hinkler was now in Florence, in a room of the Aero Club prepared as a chapel. Leading civil and military figures, including the Duke of Aosta, were among a continuous stream of Italians passing the bier and paying their respects to the aviator. The Italian state funeral, preparations for which had been proceeding apace, was but hours away.

Among the first reports to be published in England was a statement by the solicitor, L.V. Pearkes, that Bert Hinkler would probably be buried where he fell. Pearkes was sure Hinkler would rather rest there. "If anyone hated a lot of fuss it was Hinkler," the solicitor was quoted as saying. He said he was acting on the authority of a relative of Hinkler's. Pearkes had moved with alacrity on hearing the news and was already scheduled to reach Florence by the first available train, on Sunday, 30 April. He had also notified British authorities that all funeral arrangements were in his hands and that Hinkler's body would not be removed from Italy. This information was advised to the British Embassy in Rome before Pearkes arrived in Florence.

A quite different point of view was put by one of Hinkler's closest friends, Jack Savage. It was reported in Australia in the following form:

> Major Savage told the *Daily Mail* that Hinkler apparently struck a mountain when coming down to see where he was. He added that he was sure the Aero Club would assist in bringing the body to England to enable a fitting burial to be given and homage paid by his admirers. He added that Hinkler was a great aviator and a thorough gentleman. He did great things modestly and endeared himself to everyone [*Sunday Mail*, 30 April 1933, the Sunday edition of the Brisbane *Daily Mail*].

The interests of the Australian government were represented in Florence by the British consul, Major Maclean. He had been made aware, by telephone and telegram from London, of the intentions of the Australian government. These intentions ran counter to the position adopted by the solicitor. Pearkes brushed aside suggestions that the funeral be delayed and informed Maclean that the funeral should go ahead at the date and hour fixed by the Italian authorities. All others had indicated a wish that Hinkler's body be returned to the land of his birth, Australia, or to the place of his greatest achievements, England, but Pearkes was clearly marching to a different drummer. The tune of that drummer had four clearcut themes, and Pearkes himself made these themes explicit: Pearkes was in charge of funeral arrangements, the body was to be buried quietly, it was to be buried quickly, and it was to be buried permanently. Mussolini, however, though innocent of any intention to thwart Pearkes, had certainly put paid to any idea that Bert Hinkler was going to be disposed of quietly and without "a lot of fuss," as Pearkes intended.

The posture adopted by the solicitor proved unnecessary in a second respect. Under Italian law the state of decomposition of the body made immediate burial imperative in any case, and the body could not be exhumed until October, at the end of the Italian summer. Pearkes had shown his hand somewhat prematurely and unnecessarily. Major Maclean advised London of the position adopted by the solicitor and London advised Australia.

At 6:00 P.M. on 1 May, the coffin was placed in a horse-drawn hearse and the funeral procession began wending its way from the Aero Club through crowded city streets. The route it was to follow was along Via Martelli, Via Calzaioli, the Piazza Vittorio Emanuele, Via Strozzi, Via Tornabuoni, and Via Maggio, to the Piazza Santa Felicita. A band was present, two companies of infantry, one company from the Regia Aeronautica, one company of Fascist militia, and two officers from each of the various directorates and units. There were four pall bearers: General Liotta, representing General Balbo; Gen. Gino Poggesi; the prefect of Florence; and Colonel Stevens, the military attaché at the British Embassy.

Immediately behind the hearse as it passed through the streets of the city came the English clergy followed by the British consul and the solicitor L. V. Pearkes, leading members of the British community in Florence, and Italian civil and military authorities. Silent, respectful crowds lined the streets, which had earlier been placarded by the Aero Club with signs reading:

The Reserve personnel of the Regia Aeronautica and all the members of the Aero Club salute the body of the glorious British aviator Herbert John Hinkler, flyer of the Atlantic, who fell while attempting to carry out a sublime task in the service of civilisation and progress.

At the gates of the city the escort opened out, halted, and presented arms. The Fascist rite was carried out. Hinkler's name was called, and the response given: "Present." The cortege passed through and began the journey to the Cimitero degli Allori.

In the presence of Colonel Stevens, L. V. Pearkes, Major Maclean, and Captain Cottarelli—the latter of whom had accompanied the coffin from Strada—and members of the British community, the remains of the Australian aviator were interred in the soil of Italy.

Following the funeral the London solicitor proceeded to Rome and called at the offices of the Italian Air Ministry. His purpose, it was stated, was to thank the authorities for the magnificence of their tribute. During the visit to Rome he enquired for the passport that had been found on Hinkler's body. He learned from the British authorities that it was in their hands and that he would receive it in London in due course.

Pearkes left Rome for London on 3 May.

# Hinkler May Be Buried Whe

## ON "INFERNO" MOUNTAIN.

### An Ill-Fated, Storm-Swept Height Mentioned By Dante.

### PRAYING WOMEN.

### Body Lying In State In Village Church.

"THE STAR" learns that the body of Squadron-Leader Bert Hinkler will probably be buried on the spot where he was found, in the mountain wilds of Tuscany.

His friends feel that burial in such a solitary place, on the straight line of his route to Australia, would have been his wish.

**WIFE TO DECIDE.**

"I think it most probable that Mr. Hinkler will be buried in Italy, and not in either England or Australia," Mr. L. V. Pearkes, his solicitor, told a "Star" reporter to-day.

"I am sure he would rather rest where he fell than anywhere else.

"If anyone buried a lot of fuss it was Hinkler."

Mr. Pearkes is leaving London to-day to catch the Rome Express for Florence. He is in communication with Mrs. Hinkler in Australia. She, of course, who will decide where her husband is to be buried.

**BODY IN VILLAGE CHAPEL.**

Wrapped in an Italian Tricolour, with candles burning at the head and foot, the body of Hinkler is lying in state in the mortuary chapel of the church of the little village of Castello, San Niccolo, on the slope of the Appenines, says Reuter from Florence.

Soldiers and "Black Shirts," with bowed heads, kept vigil all night.

The village people have brought little bunches of wild flowers and placed them all round the bier. Many women prayed beside the body.

Search was made for a Union Jack in which to wrap the body, but none could be found, so the Italian flag was used.

**ILL-FATED MOUNTAIN.**

Hinkler met his death 4,000 feet from the summit of a mountain which is believed by the country folk to be ill-fated and haunted by evil spirits.

Peasants shun it, and only charcoal burners occasionally climb its sombre slopes.

Usually the mountain top is wreathed in clouds, and highland storms break over it. On such a day it is believed the accident occurred.

Even since the days of Dante the mountain has had its evil reputation, and in his "Inferno" Dante refers to its awe-inspiring storms. It is 4,600 feet high.

Hinkler was probably flying low in the storm to locate a landmark, and without realising his peril crashed into the mountain side.

Star (U.K.) 29.4.33

---

## MAY BE BURIED HERE

## DEAD AIRMAN

## MRS. HINKLER TO DECIDE

### GOVERNMENT OFFER

### MR. LYONS' SYMPATHY

CANBERRA, Sunday.—If it is the wish of Mrs. Bert Hinkler that the body of her husband should be brought back to Australia for burial, the Commonwealth Government will do all it can to facilitate the arrangements.

A STATEMENT to this effect was made to-night by the Prime Minister (Mr. J. A. Lyons), who said that arrangements were being made on behalf of the Commonwealth Government for Mrs. Hinkler to be met on the arrival of the Strathaird at Fremantle to-morrow, and her wishes as to the burial of her husband would then be ascertained.

**MRS. BERT HINKLER**

**AUSTRALIA'S SORROW.**

Although, as a long time had elapsed since he was last heard of, Mr. Lyons added, it was generally accepted that Mr. Hinkler had met his death on his flight from England to Australia, the news of the finding of his body would bring home to everyone very poignantly the tragic loss which Australia, in particular, and aviation in general, had suffered. The deepest sympathy of all Australians would be extended to Mrs. Hinkler and the dead airman's relatives.

Mr. Lyons has sent the following message to Mrs. Hinkler:—

"On behalf of the Government, I extend to you deepest sympathy in the tragic news of the finding of your husband's body. Australia will share your feelings of sorrow."

### "PROPER THING"

### BRING BODY BACK

### PREMIER TO CO-OPERATE

"I believe it would be the proper thing to bring his body back to Australia so that that great aviator may be accorded the honour to which his achievements

Brisbane Daily Mail 1.5.33

---

## HINKLER.

## Burial in Brisbane.

### WISH OF WIDOW.

### State Funeral to be Held.

CANBERRA, Monday.
The body of Mr. Bert Hinkler is to be buried in Brisbane. It is the wish of the aviator's widow.

The Commonwealth Government will bear the expense of having Mr. Hinkler's body brought back to Australia, and will arrange a State funeral in Brisbane.

The airman's widow, who is travelling to England by the Strathaird, expressed her wishes about funeral arrangements to a representative of the Commonwealth Government who met her to-day. The Prime Minister (Mr. Lyons) was informed, and after a meeting of the Cabinet to-night, he announced the Government's intentions.

Mr. Lyons said that final arrangements would not be made until Mrs. Hinkler reached England.

**WIDOW AND MOTHER.**

FREMANTLE, Monday.
Mr. Hinkler's widow and his mother met at Fremantle to-day. His widow heard of the finding of the body while on the liner Strathaird on Saturday afternoon. The mother heard the news at Cook, while she was on the Great Western express travelling to Perth.

**TEMPORARY BURIAL.**

LONDON, May 1.
The body of Mr. Hinkler is in Florence. It was taken there yesterday, with a guard consisting of Air Force officers and men, and the British Consul. It lies in state at the Aero Club's headquarters.

According to the British United Press, the burial has been arranged for 6 p.m. to-day. The body of the airman will be temporarily buried in the Protestant cemetery, until it has been decided when it is to be sent to Australia.

Italy is honouring Mr. Hinkler as though he were an Italian. A guard of honour, consisting of local Fascisti and members of the Italian Aero Club, watched over the flag-covered bier at Strada.

A Union Jack could not be found, so the women of Strada fashioned one by cutting strips from coloured sheets, and this covered the coffin.

Amateur musicians of Strada spent many hours on Saturday and yesterday practising the British National Anthem in order to play it while the hearse proceeded to Florence.

The Rome correspondent of the "Daily Telegraph" says that Mr. Hinkler's map showed that he intended to go a few degrees east from Florence to set a course for Brindisi, but actually he must have turned due east and encountered the Apennine range immediately after leaving the Arno River valley, instead of attempting to cross it 80 miles farther away.

The "Daily Telegraph" publishes a telegraphed picture of the wreckage of Mr.

Sydney Morning Herald 2.5.33

# Pratomagno—Forty Years Later

A              B              C              D

**A** Marino Massini. Placed markers on 1933 sites in 1974.
**B** Maria Luisa Milosh. Assisted with translations in 1974.
**C** Marshal Romeo Aureli, who was in charge of carabinieri on Pratomagno in 1933.
**D** Dr. A. M. Droandi. Arranged replacement memorial cairn on Pratomagno in 1968.

Kevin Lindeberg, right, visited Pratomagno in 1974 and, as guest of the duke of Aosta, met survivors of the 1933 events. Left to right: Gino Tocchioni, duke of Aosta, Australian ambassador John Ryan, Aladino Fabbrini, Dr. Domenico Vettori, the son of forester Adamo Gambineri, Dr. Amerigo Pispoli, and Kevin Lindeberg. The occasion was a ceremony organised by the duke; the four pictured singly above were also among those present. A project designed to elicit information from mountain villagers who participated in 1933 events came to its conclusion at this ceremony. On the same date an Arezzo representative attended a ceremony in Brisbane. His period as president of the Arezzo Aero Club had stimulated the Duke's interest in Bert Hinkler. In 1983 he organised fiftieth-anniversary ceremonies.

# 7

# PRATOMAGNO, PISA, AND POLITICS

The official enquiry set up by the Italian authorities at Strada-in-Casentino in April to record evidence connected with Hinkler's death completed its work within a few days. Its purpose was not to examine features of the disaster concerned with aerial matters but rather to document the fact that Bert Hinkler, a foreigner, died as the result of various injuries sustained in an aircraft crash. As to the reasons for the crash, there was one witness, mute though it was, that could tell all. It lay 261 metres in altitude below the summit of Pratomagno. But it was of no interest to the April enquiry.

In 1933 events moved swiftly. A comprehensive record of the facts known to all the first eye witnesses at the crash scene was never compiled, though the newspaper *La Nazione* did place some first-hand accounts on record, as did the official enquiry. The available information was not integrated. More than forty years passed before further investigations brought to light the evidence of additional key witnesses of the 1933 events. In 1974, also, some exact measurements were taken for the first time—the altitude at which the wrecked aircraft and body lay and the distance separating them. This established that the body of Hinkler was found at a height of 1,330 metres or more than 4,000 feet.

The story told by the wreckage was clear.

Hinkler had not crashed head-on into the mountain. Nor had the Puss Moth lost a wing in midair and then fallen onto the spot where it was found. Witnesses knew that the wing was attached to the aircraft when it struck a tree well down the mountainside below the summit and that this occurred subsequent to the aircraft having crossed the mountain crest.

Pratomagno, the highest point in the vicinity, stood at an altitude of 1,593 metres. It overlooked, to the north, the Hill of the Wolf, which was 1,515 metres high. The main body of wreckage lay on the Casentino side of the spine at 1,332 metres. Some distance up the mountainside, above the main wreck, lay the left wing of the aircraft beside the tree that had knocked it off. Material from "the luggage compartment" was found with the wing. This included, according to Tocchioni, Hinkler's large suitcase. Those first on the scene provided the details. *Carabiniere* Giovanni Polini reported:

At about 150 metres from the plane we found a piece of wing, other small debris, fourteen geographical maps, one shoe, one pneumatic boat, a yellow tin, a pump, and other pieces of iron. We transported the lot and reunited it with the plane.

Giuseppe Ghedini described what happened in the moments following the impact of the wing with the tree that caused this material to shower from the cabin:

Following this impact I believe that the aeroplane was still able to pursue its flight for a little while, but then it was hurled down vertically to the earth so that the propeller and a part of the engine ran into the ground. . . .

Dr. Amerigo Pispoli was a trained observer. He inspected the cockpit area and found no trace of blood. Bert Hinkler's body was at some distance—he estimated forty metres—along the mountainside from the main wreckage, and Pispoli had no doubt that Hinkler had survived the crash, made his way from the wreckage, then composed himself on the ground. There death overtook him. The Puss Moth had not collided head-on with the mountain. Coming from the Valdarno side, it passed over the mountain well below the summit of Pratomagno. It then descended the Casentino slope:

The plane did not collide against the mountain nor was it passing over its highest spot. Coming from Valdarno it was about 300 metres below the [nearby] summit, almost touching the mountain crest. Descending about 100 metres it struck a beech tree with the left wing: the wing itself naturally remained at the same spot and the plane itself fell another 150 metres down from the point of contact with the beech tree while the body of the aviator himself was

## Photo Comparison of Main Wreckage

A view of the wreckage from the engine, nearest camera, to the tail. Note the woody bush hard up against the engine and cowling. The aircraft did not slide after it struck the ground.                                                                 *D. Cosci*

With the bush removed it is evident that a propeller blade is missing from the hub assembly (A). The blade was lost while the aircraft was airborne; otherwise it would have been trapped by the bush. The remaining blade appears undamaged. That the spark from the magneto had been fully retarded is evident from the cam ring (B), a clear indication in the circumstances that the engine was off when the emergency landing was attempted.                                              *D. Cosci*

# Cam Ring Positions

Fully Retarded

Normal Running

retrieved some 40 metres away from the plane. [The distance between Hinkler's body and the wreck was measured at 80 metres in 1974.]

Aladino Fabbrini of Cetica arrived at the crash scene during the early hours following its discovery. He recalled: "It was also a beech tree with the tip broken off which cut the left wing so that it was found at a distance from the aeroplane."

Tocchioni, Ghedini, Pispoli, and Fabbrini all knew that Hinkler did not crash head-on into the mountain but had been descending the Casentino slope close to the treetops when the wing struck a larger tree. Polini, as well as the others, knew that items from inside the aircraft, as well as part of the fuselage, fell to the ground and were deposited beside the wing. Because of the steepness of the slope and the momentum of the machine, the rest of the aircraft had fallen 150 metres farther down the mountainside.

The newspaper *La Nazione* printed a detailed account:

> Far off more than 100 metres a wing lay in such a way as to indicate that its loss occurred when it was fractured by striking against one of the few beech trees in that place, resulting in the fall of the aeroplane so that it struck at a tangent against the ground throwing the pilot more than 50 metres in front.
>
> The propeller broken in half was semi-fixed to the soil and the motor sloped to the left side. The tail was the only part of the aircraft which mostly kept its characteristics. . . .

The essential facts were correctly reported, but two points need comment. The propeller stated to have been "broken in half" was actually a two-bladed metal propeller of which one blade was missing. As for Hinkler's body, a photograph makes it conclusive that he lay down and composed himself on the ground; he was some eighty metres in front of the wreckage but had not been thrown from the crashing aircraft.

While those earliest on the scene knew what the situation was, events moved fast and later arrivals received false impressions. In the twenty-one hours between Tocchioni making the discovery and the arrival of the first official party, the large suitcase he had seen beside the wing, with its contents intact, also had disappeared. It was never sighted again.

The movements of the aircraft, as attested by the wreckage, were strange indeed. Dr. Amerigo Pispoli, inquisitive to know the facts, carried out his own investigations on the Casentino slope. There were four certain indicators. At the lowest height there was a petrol tank. Next, proceeding upwards, was Hinkler's body. Above, and away from the body, there was the main wreckage stretched out from engine to tail. Higher again was the wing that had been knocked off, together with the items that fell from the cabin. He found these four indicators to be in a straight line. He projected that line upwards to where the treeline began and discovered the fifth reference point for himself. On checking the surrounds where the treeline began just below the spine, he found evidence of the aircraft's passage. Small saplings no thicker than a man's wrist had been knocked down in the onrush of the aircraft.

The final movements of the Puss Moth were now clear. They began on the Valdarno side of the mountains and ended some hundreds of metres down the Casentino slope. The point over the valley of the Arno where the aircraft turned towards the mountains, calculated by flying time, was approaching twelve minutes from Florence, very close to 11:17 A.M. local time. Prior to that, apart from fog and cloud, the flight had been an untroubled one. Why then had Hinkler deviated so suddenly from his chosen route over the Arno?

The answer is provided by photographs, more particularly two photographs, of the wreckage taken by Donatello Cosci. These provide evidence on several significant features. The first is that the wreckage landed in a cleared area encircled by trees in such a manner as to make evident that the aircraft fell there. The second is that, in the final fall of the aircraft, the right wing was pointing virtually straight downwards and the aircraft fell on its right side. The third point is equally clear: the main body of the aircraft wreckage was well down the mountainside and not near the summit.* The fourth is that the aircraft had lost one blade of its two-piece metal propeller while it was still airborne. The fifth is that the engine power had been so retarded by the pilot as to indicate

*For aerial views of the crash site see Appendix 5.

that the engine was off while the aircraft was still in the air, long before the crash.

When all the facts are put together the final minutes of Bert Hinkler's flight can be stated with fair accuracy.* From Florence he set a course over the valley of the Arno River. As the time neared 11:17 A.M.—seven hours and seven minutes from takeoff—there was a sudden roughness in the running of the motor. Instantly Hinkler throttled the motor back to fully retard the spark and in the same split second switched the motor off. As the propeller stopped revolving there was a sudden momentary shaking of the aircraft. One blade had separated from the propeller assembly. Had the blade separated when the engine was under normal power, the unbalanced propeller would have pulled the engine from the aircraft instantly. Hinkler was left in doubt as to the extent of damage to the engine mountings by the last spasm of the motor turning the unbalanced propeller. He kept the nose of his aircraft up as far as he could while still holding a flying angle. In clear view to his left at some distance was Pratomagno. There was room at the top for a landing. Hinkler was at the mercy of the wind and knew that his height and gliding speed were insufficient to reach the summit. Where the spine of the mountain met Pratomagno below the summit there was a chance. It was treeless near the spine and had what looked like a fairly steep slope, not a site he would have chosen for an emergency landing but it was the only one available. Between his aircraft and this site was Poggio del Lupo, the Hill of the Wolf.

Hinkler floated the Puss Moth sideways in a slow descent, drifting it onto the mountain. It was all over in a split-second succession of events. As the top of the mountain ridge came up to meet him, he straightened his aircraft, passed over the ridge at an angle, and possibly touched his wheels on the grassed slope as it fell away on the far side. He had to put his left wing down

*Circumstances which must be taken into account include: The possibility of fog and mist in the mountain valleys and over part of the valley of the Arno; the fierceness and direction of the winds that beat upon Pratomagno; the limitations upon Hinkler's choice by the mountain ridges in relation to his line of flight; the steepness and conjunction of the mountain ridges where he descended; the fact his engine was off; and the state of individual parts of the aircraft, which postulate the unique set of conditions which Hinkler suddenly encountered in the air.

62

to match the fall of the land; the alternative was to impact or overturn. The landing speed, the wind, and the slope caused the Puss Moth to continue airborne. Swirling winds rocked the powerless monoplane. The Puss Moth rushed across the slope towards the treeline. Hinkler straightened up again and the machine knocked over some small saplings on the edge of a steeper fall. The aircraft became airborne in open space. There was a momentary and sudden silence then the large struts holding the left wing impacted on a tall tree that stood above the others. There was a horrible tearing and rending as part of the side of the aircraft was ripped out and the wing was torn off. The aircraft continued its forward momentum but swung violently over onto its right side, with the right wing pointing downwards. The machine dropped vertically down the face of the mountain and fell into a clear space encircled by trees. As it hit the ground there was much rending and crashing and the structure disintegrated. In great pain Bert Hinkler staggered from the wreckage, his left foot shoeless. Far below across the mountain ridges he had seen the roofs of a village. The eighty metres he walked from the wreckage were an agony of movement. Unable to continue he pulled his flying coat about him and lay on the ground on the lower side of a bush. He crossed his shoeless left leg over his right. In that posture, composed as for sleep, he succumbed to his injuries. The weather was freezing. Within a few days the snow covered all.

The propeller had been manufactured in the United States by the Hamilton Standard Company. It was made up of two metal blades that were locked together at the hub by metal plates and clamping rings. Though metal propellers had been in use for some years—Hinkler himself had used a one-piece metal blade on the Avro Avian he flew from England to Australia in 1928—their use on light aeroplanes by private pilots was far from common. Normally, a private pilot could be expected to have his aircraft equipped with a wooden propeller. A broken wooden propeller on the crashed aircraft would have been in no way unusual. A failure to distinguish between the characteristics of the two types was probably the reason for the unusual events that were to follow. Investigators noted the condition of the propeller assembly, but it did not arouse their suspicions.

On 2 May 1933, the day after the funeral in Florence, a recovery party ascended the slopes of Pratomagno. It consisted of an air force squad from the station at Pisa under the command of Captain Gabrielli, reinforced by a volunteer group from Strada-in-Casentino. The story was told in *La Nazione*:

> Yesterday, in the early morning, came to Strada from the Airport S. Giusto of Pisa a squad of airmen under the command of Captain Gabrielli, with a lorry, to retrieve the wreckage of Hinkler's aircraft.
>
> The recovery party included the Podesta cav. Bussotti, the Secretary of the Fascists Mr. Zaccheria, Marshal Aureli, the photographer Cosci, various fascists, and a vanguard of junior fascists as they set off to the place of the disaster.
>
> Before they began the operation of dismantling the wreckage and recovering what, in the judgement of Captain [Gabrielli] seemed useful and important, the large company made a devout and meditative pause on the spot where the body of the brave aviator had lain, afterwards driving in a cross, which the captain carried to the spot, to leave a mark as a remembrance of the dramatic event.
>
> In the evening the motor lorry loaded with fragments returned to the village where Captain Gabrielli took a brief rest before departing for Pisa, after having left as a souvenir with the Fascists of Strada, who were of great assistance in this sad affair, the half of the propeller of Hinkler's aircraft which was found infixed in the earth at the site of the disaster.

The trophy was given a place of honour and displayed with the Australian flag in the Casa del Fascia. The propeller blade, however, was not the only memento of Hinkler's crash to remain in the district. Many parts of the aeroplane, including the engine controls, were in private hands in the villages around the mountain. Little more than the framework of the machine reached Pisa. It was to be examined in an endeavour to establish the cause of the crash. As one interested official wryly put it, "The result of this investigation is not likely to be, for various reasons, of great value."

Whether of value or otherwise, the result did not issue for six months or more. Behind the scenes, between May and December 1933, there was a clear but unstated disagreement on the cause of the crash between the Italian investigator and his British counterpart.

There were unusual aspects to the crash, apart from the state of the wreckage. Bert Hinkler was an Australian and he was flying a British-built, Canadian-registered aircraft from England to Australia when it crashed in Italy. Each aircraft has to be issued with a certificate of airworthiness; without such certificate an aeroplane is not authorised to take to the air. The certificate of airworthiness for the Puss Moth should have been Canadian because the aircraft bore a Canadian registration CF-APK. Hinkler had prepared the Puss Moth for the flight in Britain and it was inspectors of the British Aeronautical Inspection Directorate who actually carried out the examination of his machine. When the wreckage reached Pisa the Italian authorities invited a representative of the British AID to inspect the remnants of the aircraft. The man who arrived from London was Maj. J. S. Buchanan.

Prior to Hinkler's departure from England there had been a spate of Puss Moth accidents that had as their cause the wing of the aircraft contorting and separating under stress. That Hinkler intended to make a long international flight in his Puss Moth was known, so there was a double reason for the AID inspectors to give his aircraft a thorough going over. This they had done. All the modifications ordered by the Air Ministry to overcome the wing problem had been incorporated in Hinkler's aircraft. The inspectors therefore possessed a thorough and particular knowledge of the machine that had crashed in Italy. When the Italian air force officer, in endeavouring to find a cause for the crash in the remnants of the aircraft that had arrived at Pisa, came to the conclusion that Hinkler's crash was simply the latest in a series of crashes attributable to wing failure, he expressed a view with which Buchanan would find it difficult to concur. On 17 May, at Pisa, Buchanan took possession of the wing root fitting, on which suspicion would automatically fall if the Italian opinion was correct, and had it sent to England. The fact that the fitting had not split was considered by the Italians as proof that the wing had separated in flight. That the falling aircraft did not strike the trees surrounding the main wreckage was generally acknowledged, and this was regarded as further substantiation of the Italian viewpoint because it seemed to eliminate the possibility that the wing had been smashed from the aircraft.

The fallacy lay in the assumption that Hinkler was flying

straight and level. This implied that, after the wing had separated from the fuselage in midair, the rest of the aircraft then simply fell into the midst of the trees where it was found without striking any, and at the same height on the mountainside as the wing. But the wing that came off was found on the mountainside above the trees surrounding the main wreckage and not at the same level as the rest of the aircraft, as the Italian officer believed, and this wing had separated from the aircraft when it struck a tree—it did not break away in midair. Hinkler had been gliding down the face of the mountain, not flying straight and level.

Before the end of May, Major Buchanan was asked for an urgent decision. He did not give one. It was to be almost six months later before he enquired, at the request of the Aeronautical Research Committee of the National Physical Laboratory, as to the circumstances in which the wing had been found. The wreckage was much overdue for destruction by this time under Italian regulations. They had been most forebearing.

Buchanan's silence on such a comparatively simple matter over such a long period raises a number of questions. To what extent was he influenced by the fact that the Italian authorities had gone out of their way to honour Hinkler and that any disputation arising from technical points concerning the wreckage might develop into a point of national honour and be disruptive of the good relations that had been engendered? Even at the point in time when he obtained possession of the wing root fitting, a well-developed proposal had been put forward by the Arezzo Aero Club to create an impressive memorial to Hinkler on the crest of the mountain overlooking the crash site. The climate of Italian opinion was highly sympathetic. It was not the kind of climate in which to raise a dispute over interpretation of the wreckage, particularly as the British had no independent means of establishing the disposition of the wreckage as it was when originally discovered on the mountainside. Above and beyond these considerations was the more oblique question of international affairs. Such issues were beyond Buchanan's official province, but he would have been aware, as a citizen of common sense, that Germany had recently elevated to power a dictator named Adolf Hitler. This event would have reinforced any reluctance Buchanan felt at disturbing the good Anglo-Italian relations generated by Mus-

Sir John Buchanan

*R. Aero. Soc.*

solini's response to Bert Hinkler's death.

On his part the Italian investigator was quite simply unaware of the evidence taken by the April enquiry into Hinkler's death and was also mistakenly informed on the pattern of wreckage distribution. His impression that the wing had fallen to the ground a considerable distance from the aircraft and at the same level was greatly at variance with the certain knowledge of Tocchioni, Pispoli, and others. When he replied to the British he did so on the basis of his own viewpoint, which he considered established, remarking quite incidentally in respect to the state of the fallen aircraft that one blade of the propeller was missing, and that the aircraft did not slide when it struck the ground.

Eventually the solicitor L. V. Pearkes was approached by the Air Ministry for consent to the long-postponed destruction of the wreckage. In giving approval, Pearkes said that "Both Mrs. Hinkler and myself were under the impression that this had been done some time ago."

The result of the central issue being left unresolved became evident several years later. The final British statement on the crash of CF-APK, number 1699 in the official Reports and Memoranda series, recorded that "The Italian authorities gave it as their opinion . . . " that the crash was caused by wing failure. The general impression given by this British document (though nowhere expressly stated in it) was that British authorities concurred with the Italian opinion. There was no mention of the presence of Maj. J. S. Buchanan nor of the reasons he refrained from expressing his opinion.

A myth was thereby created that—because it appeared to have the support of British opinion—became self-perpetuating. Many years later, after a distinguished career, Major Buchanan became Sir John Buchanan. He was a man of high reputation on the engineering side of aviation.

Bert Hinkler's Puss Moth did not crash because of wing failure. It crashed when Hinkler attempted an emergency landing. The emergency occurred in the air at some distance from the final crash site. At the time of the landing the propeller was not revolving and the engine was off. One blade from the two-blade metal propeller assembly was missing. The manufacturer of the propeller was the Hamilton Standard Company in the U.S.A. No other propeller of that same type manufactured by that company ever experienced a similar malfunction, with one blade being ejected during flight. Hinkler demonstrably had become the victim of a most singular occurrence.

But was that occurrence simply an accident? Or was the propeller tampered with before he took off? Without the propeller available for examination, it is not possible to say. Even Bert Hinkler, had he survived, would probably not have been able to prove anything, no matter what he suspected. But if it was tampered with, someone in England must have known. Is it possible to detect foreknowledge of Hinkler's disaster in the sequence of strange events that took place in England in the hours and days surrounding his takeoff for Australia? Strange and irreconcilable many of those events certainly were, and they had become even stranger during the period the wreckage of the Puss Moth was under examination at Pisa Aerodrome.

## Structure of the Puss Moth

In the crash the left wing was knocked from the Puss Moth by a treetop and the aircraft fell to earth on its right side farther down the mountain. The right wing was crushed when the aircraft struck the ground. The left wing and other items found with it were placed with the main wreckage soon after discovery.

A. Moveable flap permitting wing fold
B. Left (port) wing
C. Right (starboard) wing
D. Left elevator and tailplane

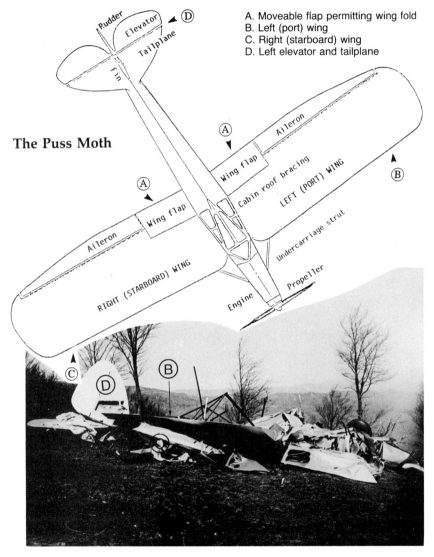

### The Puss Moth

*D. Cosci*

**Flight Commander L. V. Pearkes**

# 8

# THE INTESTATE AVIATOR

When L. V. Pearkes arrived back at his London office in Cannon Street early in May after attending Hinkler's funeral there were three major matters to be attended to. He naturally expected, after his call at the British Embassy in Rome, that all the personal items retrieved from the crash site would be forwarded to him as soon as the embassy received them from the Italian authorities. He felt a particular concern to obtain the Canadian passport, dated 18 March 1932, which was found on Hinkler's body. The matter of finalising Hinkler's estate by an application to the court based now on the certainty, rather than presumption, of Hinkler's death, had also to be put in train. There was, in addition, the question of reburial of the airman's body, on which Pearkes was being pressed by Australian authorities. Now that the excitement of the state funeral in Florence was over, the various matters could take their normal course within the quietitude of the legal system.

The British Embassy forwarded the passport to its own superiors, the Foreign Office in London, on 4 May, the day following Pearkes's departure from Italy. Pearkes expected that the passport would arrive at his office within a few days of his return, and his anxiety began to increase when more than a week passed without any word from the authorities. By 16 May he felt he had sufficient cause for concern to write to the Foreign Office. Unfortunately for him, the passport was passed to the Dominions Office the same day his letter was received, 18 May. Initially Pearkes was told, on 20 May, that the matter was being looked into, and then subsequently that the document had been dispatched elsewhere. This reply seemed to provide him with additional energy for on 25 May two letters issued from the legal firm of Pettiver &

Pearkes, one to the Dominions Office and one to the under secretary of state at the Foreign Office. The latter said:

> We are in receipt of your letter of yesterday's date which has caused us some consternation. We think it advisable to make it clear what has happened in this matter. Our Mr. Pearkes represents the relatives and when the body was found proceeded to Florence to arrange for the funeral after which he went to Rome to interview the British Ambassador about certain matters and requested the Secretary of the Embassy to send the Passport and personal effects to this country as soon as possible.
>
> On the 16th inst. we wrote to you regarding the matter and on the 20th inst. we received a reply to the effect that our letter would receive attention. You now inform us that the Passport was received a considerable time ago and was forwarded to the Dominions Office. We fail to understand why this document has gone to the Dominions Office but apart from this could we not have been informed before? We now learn that no personal effects have been received at all which we also consider we should have been told before having regard to the amount of money found on the body in addition to his presentation watch received from the Government of Australia and other articles of value.
>
> Will you please therefore let us know by return whether you propose to take this matter up with the Italian Authorities or not as it is most urgent and of the utmost importance to the relatives.
>
> We are,
> Your obedient servants,
> Pettiver & Pearkes

The letter was signed in Pearkes's handwriting but in the name of the firm. The extent of his anxiety is evident not only from his using the word "consternation" but from the fact that the letter was delivered to the Foreign Office on the day it was written. The Dominions Office replied to him on Saturday, 27 May, while the Foreign Office, which replied on Monday, 29 May, recommended he now approach Australia House to obtain the passport and request an official approach to Italy concerning the rest of Hinkler's personal effects. The passport had managed to keep just out of Pearkes's reach, but he was rapidly gaining on it. That he obtained the document very quickly from Australia House is evident from a letter that issued from that office on 1

June to the Foreign Office enquiring, on Pearkes's behalf, for the items recovered at the crash scene. It demonstrated that the solicitor had responded with alacrity to the Foreign Office suggestion, as indeed had Australia House also to his approach. The absence of any reference to the passport in the letter of 1 June implies that Pearkes had finally secured it. Strangely, despite the involvement of Australia House in the early period of Bert Hinkler's disappearance, there seems to have been no direct knowledge there of the solicitor until this time. During the disputation in Florence over the burial of Hinkler's body, it had been the London representative of the Queensland government who was in communication with Major Maclean, the British consul in Florence, not the Australian minister resident in London.

The *Strathaird* docked in the Thames on 2 June 1933. One woman passenger had had much to think of in the preceding thirty-three days. Now that Bert was dead, life would never be the same again. She would have to start a new life. Nancy knew that she faced many readjustments and looked forward to reaching her Thornhill home. She was not without relatives of her own in Yorkshire and knew also that a warm welcome awaited her from one near relative who was very dear to her.

When the press enquired from Nancy about a fortnight later concerning the reburial of Hinkler's body in Australia, Nancy replied that she was awaiting the arrival in England of Mrs. Lores Bonney, who was making a solo flight from Australia, and intended to discuss the matter with her. She had farewelled Mrs. Bonney at Brisbane in early April but there had been some major problems on the flight, one of which had made an almost complete rebuild of Mrs. Bonney's aircraft necessary in Calcutta.

In point of fact there was nothing to discuss. Almost certainly by this time Nancy had been in touch with the solicitor L. V. Pearkes and had become familiar with the situation in England. In her statement to the press, if she was correctly reported, she had simply bought time.

Pearkes's claim was that he was acting directly for Bert Hinkler. Hinkler, so it was asserted, before leaving on the flight had asked Pearkes to handle his affairs during his absence abroad. Hinkler's estate was now in the process of being finalised. Nancy had been in New Zealand when Bert took off and, for further reasons that were soon to emerge, was in a vulnerable position and unable to counter the solicitor's claims.

The application went before the Probate Court in London on 23 June and the sequel was reported in the Melbourne *Argus* and elsewhere on 27 June:

> The estate of the late Squadron-Leader Hinkler, who was killed when his aeroplane crashed in Italy, while he was flying from England to Australia, has been proved at £906 gross, the net personality being £792. As Squadron-Leader Hinkler died intestate, letters of administration have been granted to the widow.

The *Times* stated:

> Mr. Herbert John Louis Hinkler of Scholing, near Southampton, an Honorary Squadron Leader of the Royal Australian Air Force, who died in January, left estate exclusive of property in Australia and elsewhere of the gross value of £906 with net personalty £792.

Bert Hinkler received many gifts in Australia after his successful pioneering solo flight from England in 1928. Because of the unfavourable exchange rate, he invested most of the money in Australia in war bonds maturing between 1938 and 1961, and this investment, together with his Australian bank account, totalled at his death over £11,000 Australian. The American equivalent in dollars was many times that figure at that time. This element in the deceased's estate was not referred to in, nor known to, the press in June 1933, but some six months later there was a press report that Hinkler's estate was valued at more than £12,000. Special legal provisions applied to the Australian element in the estate; on the death of the widow any amount remaining was to be distributed to Hinkler's mother and the other members of his family in Bundaberg.

The personal effects of Hinkler retrieved from the crash site arrived in London and were handed to the solicitor's representative at Australia House on 27 June. Many items known to have been in Hinkler's possession on the aircraft were missing. Of particular concern was a suitcase, described as a Revelation (expanding) type, which contained, among other things, £800 in bond receipts. Also missing was the gold watch presented by the Australian government and a gold cigarette case. In monetary terms these had greater value than the possessions that had been returned. As it seemed possible that the items had been mislaid or misdirected in Italy, enquiries to establish the position were authorised by Australia House immediately. This, in due course, elicited a response to the effect that all items retrieved from the wreckage had been returned to England.

The matters that had so agitated Pearkes almost from the moment that the first reports of the discovery of Hinkler's body and wrecked aircraft reached England—the Canadian passport and the personal effects—were now safely, if not satisfactorily, finalised. The major legal matter, Hinkler's estate, had passed through the Probate Court. It seemed that Pearkes's connection with Hinkler's affairs was nearing its end.

In the application to the Probate Court, Pearkes had described himself as "an intimate friend of the deceased." While Bert Hinkler had many friends and a legion of admirers of his flying skill, there were very few indeed who would be so bold as to describe themselves as his "intimate friend." In the doubt and confusion in the days following Hinkler's disappearance this had been made particularly clear. On what grounds could such a claim by the solicitor rest?

Bert Hinkler and Leslie Pearkes came from quite dissimilar backgrounds. The Australian was born into a working-class family in 1892, Pearkes in London in 1895, the son of a solicitor. Hinkler's education began in January 1898 at North Bundaberg State School, and during his school days, when he was able, he made some pocket money for himself by delivering newspapers around the local districts before school. He found employment at the age of thirteen, working in a bicycle shop in Bundaberg and in a photographic studio in nearby Gympie, where his grandparents resided. As a youth he earned something of a name for himself in Bundaberg with a camera. He worked in the Bundaberg Foundry and at the Qunaba Sugar Mill, finding time to design and build two monoplane gliders. Self-reliance and an independent, inquisitive attitude on matters pertaining to flight became dominant Hinkler characteristics. By the age of nineteen a visiting itinerant aerial showman, an American airman named Arthur Burr Stone, recognised Hinkler's ability and gave him a job as an assistant during a tour of Victoria and New Zealand in late 1912 and 1913. Hinkler worked his passage to England in 1914 and there obtained a job with the Sopwith Aviation Company "on the bench" until the war broke out in 1914, when he joined the Royal Naval Air Service.

Pearkes joined the Royal Naval Air Service too, but in 1915. His father, Arthur Edward Pearkes, was a partner in a London firm of solicitors, Pettiver and Pearkes, and Leslie Vincent Pearkes spent some time with the firm before enlisting. His schooling took place at Neville House, Eastbourne, and at Chigwell School in Essex. His entry into the RNAS was as an observer, but he soon became a pilot, receiving his first instruction from Jack Alcock who, in 1919, was to gain fame with Arthur Whitten Brown as the first to cross the Atlantic by aeroplane.

It was at Luxeuil in Belgium in 1916 that Pearkes met Hinkler. They were serving on the same squadron, Hinkler as a gunner and Pearkes as a pilot, though they never flew as a team. The squadron also operated from Ochey. After a year's service at the front, Pearkes was posted back to England. Hinkler remained until the end of 1917, when he was posted to Greenwich for training as a pilot. When flying as a gunner with a Canadian, C. B. Sproatt, on operations in a DH4, Hinkler had been given an opportunity to try himself at the controls. He so impressed Sproatt with his handling of the aircraft that he was recommended for pilot training. Hinkler then served in 1918 at various training establishments, including Marske in Yorkshire. (By this time his relationship with Nancy, who was a nurse, had already matured. Wounded in France and hospitalised in England, Jack Hinkler, the airman's brother, had known Nancy while he was in hospital, though whether this was before or after Bert met her, or whether it may even have been the cause of their meeting, is uncertain.) During the same period the Royal Flying Corps and the Royal Naval Air Service amalgamated to form the Royal Air Force. There was a war going on in Italy against the Austrians and Hinkler was posted there to 28 Squadron, Royal Air Force, remaining until the Armistice was signed. Pearkes became a solicitor in 1921 and a partner in the practice in 1926 when his father died. He did no flying after World War I; Hinkler, however, went on to make aviation his career.

When Bert Hinkler took off from the Great West Aerodrome on 7 January 1933, his immediate destination was Australia. To reach that country in his single-engined monoplane he would cross deserts, mountains, jungles, and long stretches of water. If forced down, he would find that facilities had improved since his solo flight of 1928 but only marginally. There was still no established air route through to what was known as the Far East; some two years were to elapse before that took place. After a period with his family in Bundaberg, he intended to fly from Australia to Canada, presumably around the rim of Asia. Hinkler had taken quite extraordinary steps to retain the Canadian registration of his aircraft, CF-APK, his request only being granted because of an error by the official handling the application. Resolving this issue had been one of the causes of the delay in his departure from England.

Such a flight in a single-engined aircraft was replete with danger. Strange, then, that though Hinkler was said to have appointed a solicitor before taking off on the flight, he left no record of having done so and, moreover, was eventually found to have died intestate.

Throughout his activities as Hinkler's solicitor, Pearkes had often asserted that he was speaking on behalf of Hinkler's "relatives." Just what that term was meant to imply was about to become evident when the matter of reburial came to an issue. It certainly did not include Bert Hinkler's mother or the family in Bundaberg.

# Lt. Bert Hinkler

Name: Herbert John Louis Hinkler
Birth: 8 December 1892, Bundaberg, Queensland
Enlisted: Royal Naval Air Service, 7 September 1914, as mechanic
Served: England, France, Belgium, Italy.
Awards: Distinguished Service Medal (1917), Air Force Cross (1928)
Demobilised: 1919, 2d Lieutenant, pilot, Royal Air Force
Promoted: Honorary Squadron Leader, RAAF, March 1928

# The Propeller—"Karohi" at Hendon

The manner in which the propeller blades are locked into place at the hub with metal plates and clamping rings can be seen in this photo taken outside the Skywriting hangar at Hendon. Note also the arrow and the unusual name Hinkler gave to his aircraft. *M. Allen*

*9*

# OUT OF THE SHADOWS

On 8 September 1933, the *Sydney Morning Herald* published a report from Brisbane:

## MR. BERT HINKLER
## BODY TO REMAIN IN ITALY

"Mrs. Hinkler and I have come to the conclusion, after consulting our lawyers, and considering the lapse of time since Bert's death, that it is better to leave the body in Italy, especially in view of the splendid memorial erected by the Italians," said Mrs. H. A. Hinkler, mother of the famous aviator, on her return today from Sydney and Western Australia.

Mrs. Hinkler said that the airman's widow was settling in Southampton [England] . . .

To the world at large it seemed that the fervour of the moment having passed—it was more than four months since the funeral—a more sober view was being taken. The key was in the reference to consulting lawyers. The genuine feelings of the family in Bundaberg were quite different. George Hinkler's attitude, expressed quite forcefully at the time of the funeral, was strongly entrenched and became even stronger over subsequent years: the body of his brother should rest in the place of his birth. The family were not in any position to sway official opinion, however, or even to indicate the reason for Frances Hinkler's statement. This point was reinforced in an unexpected way when, without any application being made by her, she received a special grant of £104 per year. The Australian government had learned she was in indigent circumstances and waived the need for a formal application. In

Australia at that time the Great Depression was blighting the land and life was hard for many Australians.

Behind the scenes in England, in July, Australian officials in London had received unusual information. It was of such a nature that it was conveyed to Australia by confidential mail personally delivered. The letter reached its destination in August and the recipient government then decided that, in view of all the circumstances, it was better that the body of the Australian aviator should remain in Florence. A minor drama was played out behind the scenes, but the public knew nothing of these background issues.

Unknown to even his closest acquaintances—and this initially included both his mother and Nancy—Bert Hinkler's domestic situation had changed dramatically when he was in the United States in 1932. The legal widow, finally forced out of the shadows by the reburial issue, was Katherine Hinkler. When Pearkes had said, at the end of January 1933, that he was acting for a "relative" of Hinkler's when he ordered the memorial service to be cancelled, and then on later occasions that he was acting for "the widow" and "relatives," the person he was really referring to was the same at all times—the legal widow, Katherine Hinkler. She was the hidden drummer when Pearkes asserted his control over the funeral in Florence.

At the end of World War I, when Hinkler remained in England instead of returning to Australia, his intention had been to marry Nancy, the nurse he'd met during the four years of violence, bloodshed, perpetual turmoil, and disruption to private lives. It seems the banns were already issued for the marriage when it was learned a legal impediment existed. The marriage could not proceed, but in all other respects Nancy and Bert continued with their plans. Nancy had a young daughter from her earlier marriage. There was a view fairly widely held by the general populace in the pioneering years of flight that men who took up flying should not marry because of the dangers of their vocation. Some justification for the attitude can be found. The attitude was at one time reflected in an official policy. Not all women would be prepared to accept a continuation of flying after marriage, and in fact, there are several fine aviators who can be named who gave up flying because of wifely attitudes. Nancy proved very supportive of Bert's role as a test pilot at Hamble and solo airman and participated with him in some of his local flying. Despite press reports to the contrary, she was aware at all times of his plans for major flights, including the 1931 crossing of the South Atlantic and, strangely enough, the flight that proved to be his last. Her departure from England for New Zealand in November 1932 meant she became uninformed on the subsequent changes to his plans in the delay that followed until his actual takeoff on 7 January. Throughout the years their union seemed to match every criterion except the legal one.

The continual separations caused by flying placed Nancy in a vulnerable position; some might say the same about Hinkler himself. According to those closest to the scene at the time, Bert Hinkler first met Katherine towards the end of 1925 when he visited the United States with the British Schneider Cup team. Nancy was older than Bert; Katherine, attractive and vivacious, nine years younger than him. The British team left England on the *Minnewaska* on 26 September 1925 for the competition in Baltimore and did not return until over a month later. They were treated like visiting potentates during their stay in the U.S.A. The Schneider Trophy race was an international competition between seaplanes built by the contending nations. The air race itself was something of a disaster for Britain, relieved only by the almost miraculous survival of British pilot Henri Biard after a descent under power straight into the sea. The reserve aeroplane, pressed into service at short notice to enable Hinkler to qualify under the rules, damaged its floats because of pressure of the waves after gales had passed. Time ran out and Hinkler was unable to compete in the race itself. The British flag was carried by the third pilot, Hubert Broad, but the American team finished easy winners, with the Italians second. Biard later mentioned the events of 1925 in his autobiography, referring to his spectacular crash and including an account of the return passage to England. There was a certain amount of horseplay by Biard, Broad, and Hinkler on that ship in exacting retribution upon a moustachioed passenger who persisted in complaining at their attempts to entertain themselves. Hinkler seemed to play a leading role, which was a departure from his normally reserved attitude. Though Hinkler never visited the United States again until late in 1930, it appears that from the first meeting onwards Katherine had some sort of hold over him, or upon him, and that their association continued.

Nancy was with Bert in the U.S.A. for part of the time during his visit in 1930–31. Late in 1931 Bert made his way back to England in his Puss Moth, making a historic solo flight from Canada to the U.S.A., thence by way of the Caribbean, South America, the South Atlantic, northwest Africa, Spain, and France to England.

It was a famous flight and it brought fame not only to Hinkler, as acknowledged by several prestigious awards, but also to his aircraft and the peculiar name he gave it—*Karohi*. Asked on several occasions what the significance of this name was, Hinkler replied that it meant "the lone hand." No doubt Hinkler was familiar with the Australian publication of the 1910 period that bore that title. In the early 1930s it became something of a practice for prominent aviators to name their aeroplanes after friends or relatives. Jim Broadbent named a sequence of machines *DABS*, after his deceased friend, the young aviator D. A. B. Smith. Jim Melrose called his Puss Moth *My Hildebrande* after his mother. C. W. A. Scott had Chinese characters inscribed on the cowling of his Gipsy Moth, about which a great deal of mystery was made: they were later said to mean "Kathleen" and to refer to Scott's wife whom he'd met in Hong Kong. Taking the "HI" in *Karohi* to stand for Hinkler, the first four letters can be seen as an abbreviation for Katherine and her maiden name, which began appropriately. Though very much oblique, this naming of the aircraft reveals a high degree of naiveté on Hinkler's part. Apparently he had no idea that the unusual name of his aircraft would arouse a lot of penetrating questions when he completed his outstanding flight.

*Karohi* remained in a hangar at Southampton when Hinkler returned to the U.S.A. on the *Majestic* in February 1932. He took his Riley car with him instead. His acquisition of a Canadian passport in March was commented on in a message to the Australian press:

## MR. BERT HINKLER
## ARCTIC FLIGHT EXPECTED

Ottawa, March 18. Mr. Bert Hinkler, the Australian airman, visited Ottawa on Friday. He would not speak of his plans, but it is known he interviewed high officials of the Royal Canadian Air Force and made arrangements for a passport from the Government. It is believed that he contemplates a flight across the North Atlantic via the Arctic route [*Argus*, 21 March 1932].

At this time it was apparently Hinkler's intention to return to England in April, at least according to press reports:

New York, April 19. Mr. Bert Hinkler, the Australian aviator, will leave for England by the *Majestic* on Saturday. Later he hopes to proceed to Australia. He said in an interview, "I have no flight plans at present." [*Sydney Morning Herald*, Thursday, 21 April 1932].

Hinkler did not return to England, but lingered on in America. There was a growing parental concern on the part of Katherine's father. The next act in the drama seems not to have been premeditated, certainly not by Bert Hinkler; more probably it was instigated by Katherine's father. In the U.S. state of Connecticut a marriage license was taken out on Monday, 16 May 1932. Five days later, on Saturday, 21 May 1932, a marriage took place before a justice of the peace. Connecticut was obviously chosen in order to minimise the possibility of recognition and publicity; Hinkler, however, thought fit to add a further subterfuge as a means of preventing detection of the marriage, a subterfuge that significantly reinforces the notion of Hinkler's naïveté in his relations with women.

Katherine's existence was no surprise to Nancy; each had been aware of the other throughout the years. But in the short period after Hinkler returned to England in September 1932 and Nancy's departure for New Zealand in November, Hinkler did not divulge to her what had occurred. Apparently Nancy was made aware only that a parting of the ways was imminent and this was the matter weighing heavily on her mind when she visited Bundaberg and the Gruter family in Brisbane. Hinkler, nevertheless, thought it advisable to inform her of the delay in his flight plans and a cable reached Nancy in New Zealand a few days before Christmas in 1932.

Hinkler's reticence on the subject of the marriage can be understood, given the circumstances. Despite the embarrassing situation in which Nancy later found herself when she learned the legal position from others, she did not then, nor subsequently, issue one public word of criticism of Hinkler. Presumably she would wish that to remain the position.

When, acting on Pearkes's application, the Probate Court granted letters of administration of Hinkler's estate to the widow, the widow in question was Katherine Hinkler. In just seven-and-a-half months Katherine had been transmogrified from legal wife to legal widow, becoming the beneficiary of Hinkler's estate under circumstances that demanded the closest scrutiny. She was one end of a secret tug-of-war that developed behind the scenes over Hinkler's body. The public impression that Nancy was the legal widow provided a very convenient cover for the activities of Katherine, whose existence remained unknown.

On 8 September 1933, at the time the announcement was made that there would be no reburial, Australia learned that the Arezzo Aero Club had completed the memorial to Hinkler on the top of the spur overlooking the crash site and that it was to be unveiled on Sunday, 17 September. The military attaché at the British Embassy in Rome, Colonel Stevens, was chosen to represent the Australian government at the ceremony.

No longer under any threat on the reburial issue, "the widow" was represented at the ceremony by solicitor Pearkes. She did not attend. Pearkes had now been involved in a number of unusual events on her behalf. On his return to England from Pratomagno, Pearkes felt sufficiently confident to write to the *Times*. The letter was published on 27 September. The widow it referred to was Katherine, but readers of the *Times* would have assumed the reference was to Nancy:

> On my return from Italy I was most interested to see in your issue of the 22nd inst. a photograph of the memorial erected by the Aero Club of Arezzo in honour of the late Squadron-Leader H. J. L. Hinkler. I attended the ceremony on the 17th inst. and on May 1 last was present at the funeral at Florence, and in these circumstances I think it is only fitting that the public should know how splendid the Italians have been in honouring the name of this famous British airman.
>
> I journeyed to Florence representing the widow immediately

I heard that the body had been found, as for three months I had been engaged in carrying on a search in France and Switzerland through various agencies. It was the wish of the widow that the funeral should be a quiet, and simple one, but on arriving in Florence I found that the body had been lying in state for 48 hours and the Italian authorities had made preparations for the burial to take place with full military honours. This was indeed an honour, and the funeral was most impressive, as anyone who has any knowledge of the sympathetic Italian temperament on these occasions will easily realize.

Not content with this touching tribute the Aero Club at Arezzo recently erected a memorial at the place where Hinkler fell. The site is over 4,500 feet high on the slopes of Pratomagno, in the Tuscan Mountains, and rarely visited because of its inaccessibility and the fact that in the winter months it is covered in snow. It was necessary to go by motor-car from Florence to Strada, beyond which place it was impossible for a car to proceed, and Colonel Stevens, the British Military Attaché in Rome, and I left Florence at 2:45 A.M. to be at Strada at 5:00 A.M., the time appointed by the Aero Club for the procession to start, this early hour being necessary to avoid the heat of the day. At Strada we were met by the President of the Aero Club, the head of the local Fascisti, and other officials. We then mounted mules, and the final journey began, lasting three hours through wild and rugged country.

The memorial itself is about 8 ft. in height, made of marble, and representing an eagle with a broken wing. The most impressive thing of all was to find that over 200 people had managed somehow or other to find their way to this outlandish spot at this hour of the morning—surely a magnificent tribute to Hinkler's memory. The people assembled then formed a circle round the memorial and short addresses were delivered by the Club President and others. The scene at the top of the mountain will not easily be forgotten because of its utter simplicity.

I consider it only right that your readers should be acquainted with the wonderful sentiment displayed by the Italian people for a British airman, the more so because nothing at all has been done in this country to perpetuate Hinkler's memory, and moreover none of the numerous flying clubs here was represented at the funeral or the memorial ceremony, and no floral tributes were even sent.

Yours very truly,
L. V. Pearkes
21 College Hill, Cannon Street, E.C.4, Sept. 25

This letter is deserving of a close analysis. Its concluding criticism is a strange one, coming as it does from a member of the Royal Aero Club, albeit one whose membership rested solely upon his wartime service. It becomes even stranger when considered against another letter written about the same time. Far from the public gaze, and carried away perhaps by overconfidence, Katherine put her own views in writing. She had informed the Australian authorities verbally on 12 September, during a visit with Pearkes to the government officials, that if she changed her views on reburial she would inform them. She was then able to use the Italian ceremony as a means of ending the reburial issue once and for all. In a letter issuing from the office of Pettiver & Pearkes and dated 2 October 1933, she said:

Since seeing you I have given much thought to the desire of your Government to learn my wishes regarding the possible removal of the body of my husband, the late Squadron-Leader H. J. L. Hinkler, from Italy to Australia for re-burial, and after careful consideration of all the circumstances I have come to the decision that I cannot permit a removal.

Some time before my husband's body was found, but when it was no longer possible to hope for other than a tragic finding, I decided that wherever he was eventually discovered was to be the scene of his burial. It seemed quite apparent to me, with the information then available, that only the most perfunctory concern was felt as to his fate—or at least no concern sufficiently great to arouse any practical activity. And since then nothing has come to me which would lead me to conclude that that information was not entirely correct. I am of course aware that the disappearance of a civilian airman is not a matter which casts any obligation on any body, official or private; and I also know the difficulties and frequent lack of success which have attended searches undertaken for other unfortunate airmen, even when such searches have had governmental co-operation. At the same time and while I had no thought that anything could or would be done for Bert Hinkler than common humanity would dictate in the case of anyone in similar trouble, it was my feeling that there could be no greater tribute, no finer gesture, than for some step to be taken which might or might not result in the finding of a man who, it was finally discovered, crashed directly on his route.

After reviewing once again all the facts, I find that it is not possible for me to put aside my personal feelings or to think otherwise than I have done during the last eight months, which is that once my husband's body had been found the time had passed when any worth-while tribute could be paid to him by any part of the British Empire.

If his name is to be remembered by future generations of Australians, I hope that remembrance will rest on whatever he achieved rather than on the place of his burial; if he is to be forgotten by those future generations, I for one shall be sorry but not surprised, for I shall remember that he was also forgotten by his own generation at a time when it might have meant his life.

Mr. L.V. Pearkes, my husband's friend, to whom, as also to M. Saby, Inspector of Forests and Waterways at Sens, I owe a lasting debt of gratitude for all that was done to trace him, has returned from his second visit to Italy—you will remember that Mr. Pearkes went to Florence at the end of April to arrange the funeral—where he was present as my representative at the dedication of the memorial erected at the instigation of the Aero Club of Arezzo on the mountain which was the scene of the crash. What he has told me of this further expression of regard has confirmed my belief that any honour which could now be paid in Australia could only be a repetition of what has already been done.

I hope you will forgive me for this very long letter, but I know that you will understand how painful a subject it is to me and how much I should like it closed once and forever.

Yours faithfully,
Katherine Hinkler

The lady protests too much. The letter is too clever by half.

There was a period in the days immediately following Hinkler's takeoff, the "time when it might have meant his life," that an authoritative voice was urgently needed to stimulate activity and to give direction and purpose to search efforts and other enquiries. No such voice arose from the tumult. It was not as though the need for such a voice went unobserved. Even more specifically, the *Daily Herald* of 10 January spoke of a woman:

An amazing position arose in England yesterday. There was no one in this country who was prepared to take the responsibility of inaugurating a search for Hinkler and his plane. Hinkler made the flight purely as a personal venture; he had no financial backers; he was using his own machine, and he had not arranged with anyone to look after his affairs. Mrs. Hinkler, the airman's wife, left England recently and is now in Australia awaiting her husband's arrival. She said last night she was not unduly worried.

IF ANYTHING HAPPENED

"My husband always turns up some time or other," she added.

I am able to reveal that Hinkler had made private arrangements with a woman friend, of himself and his wife, that if anything serious arose he would telegraph her.

This woman friend had been told to get in touch with Mr. F. Hazell Jones, an aviation expert in London. Hinkler, before he left, entirely forgot, however, to complete the final arrangements of this one and only English contact.

Last night Mr. Jones told me that he was very perturbed about Hinkler's disappearance. "I am not acting for him in any way, officially," he added. "He told me [she] would be cabled if anything urgent arose, but he did not tell me who she was."

Where was Katherine then, at the very time when it might have meant Hinkler's life?

Katherine does not occupy the moral high ground in the debate on Hinkler's disappearance, though she seeks to do so in her letter. On the contrary, she faces a lot of explaining but diverts attention from herself by making a bold attack on others. Katherine had to be literally dragged out of cover. Pearkes's letter to the *Times* concluded with a criticism of British flying clubs in an attempt to place flying clubs at a disadvantaged position in any debate on Hinkler. As he was in a privileged position because he was informed of the intended memorial ceremony well in advance of the event, and was a member of the Royal Aero Club, it would have been a simple matter for him to have drawn the club's attention to the Italian ceremony and to the means by which a memorial gesture might be made. Pearkes clearly had not done so.

The stratagems in the letters are apparent. Both Pearkes and Katherine claim the moral high ground. The important point at issue Katherine puts to rest quickly—the reburial of Hinkler's body will not be permitted. Attacking at once, she accuses others of inactivity. But this attack can be blunted and turned on her. She herself did nothing. She blocks any attempt at keeping Hinkler's memory alive in Britain; the time has already passed for such a tribute she says. There are only two persons for whom she feels a lasting debt of gratitude—the Frenchman, Monsieur P. Saby, and her husband's friend, L. V. Pearkes, solicitor. Pearkes had gone to Florence to arrange the funeral, then returned to Italy some months later as her representative at the dedication of the memorial. Katherine wishes the matter closed once and forever.

Certain themes guided the mind of the writer, and Katherine's attitude can be stated much more bluntly. Hinkler is buried and will stay buried. The subject is closed and, like Hinkler's grave, will not be reopened. Any continuation of the association between the solicitor and herself will demonstrate her lasting gratitude. Others, who are in no position to criticise, might now mind their own business. And that included the Australian government.

Administration.

## DEATH ON OR AFTER 1st JANUARY, 1898.

BE IT KNOWN that *Herbert John Louis Hinkler of Mon Repas Scholing near Southampton Hants*

died on the *7th* day of *January* 1933 *at Castel S. Nicolo Province of Arezzo in Italy*

intestate

AND BE IT FURTHER KNOWN that at the date hereunder written Letters of Administration of all the Estate which by law devolves to and vests in the personal representative of the intestate were granted by His Majesty's High Court of Justice at the Principal Probate Registry thereof to *Katherine Hinkler of 177 Falkland Mansions Glasgow Scotland* ~~of the same address~~

the lawful ~~husband~~ widow and relict of the said intestate.

Dated the *23rd* day of *June* 1933.

*Gross value of Estate* ——£ *906 – 10 – 10*

*Net value of Personal Estate* ——£ *792 - 2.2*

IIID.

# Falkland Mansions, Glasgow

Bert Hinkler's final telephone call reached a person inside this building.

## 10

# A SCORE CARD

When Bert Hinkler failed to arrive at Brindisi during the afternoon of Saturday, 7 January 1933, the possibilities were endless. Hinkler was nothing if not versatile in a crisis. He might have come down in the sea and be floating about just off the shipping lanes. There were also many remote wilderness areas in Europe, and he could have crashed in one of these, survived, and be awaiting rescue. There was a possibility he could have come down in an area where it would take several days to reach civilisation or be experiencing difficulty making himself understood to local villagers. It was not unknown for airmen to land in such places and be locked up. Such a fate had come the way of Tom Kay and G. C. Matthews in 1919 in Yugoslavia, when they were attempting a flight to Australia, and Hinkler himself came close to a similar experience in 1927 in Poland; there had also been similar type incidents elsewhere. On the other hand Hinkler may have been badly injured in the crash and been forced to await rescue or death. At such times aviators or survivors had been known to indulge in the practice of writing final messages on pieces of aircraft wreckage. Hinkler had on hand plenty of writing materials and might even have composed extended last messages in his log book or note books. Just what those last messages might say about the causes of the crash or about the domestic situation could only be conjectured. A message from the dead would certainly have had a very lively impact, given all the circumstances. Some of the papers and documents Hinkler carried on his person or in the plane might possibly have had an even greater impact. Many of these possibilities remained throughout the whole period of Hinkler's disappearance of three-and-a-half months from 7 January until 27

April and increased in importance as time passed. One, however, did not—the possibility of Hinkler's continued survival. After about 17 January his death could be regarded as a virtual certainty. He would not be reappearing.

It is against this background, and its uncertainties, that the activities of Katherine Hinkler and L.V. Pearkes can be measured. Their attempt in September and October 1933 to occupy the moral high ground, preaching moral virtue to others, provides very relevant criteria for evaluating their own conduct. It is only just that they be judged by the standards they said others should meet. But before their activities are assessed and "scored," a further enlightening incident has to be taken into account: Bert Hinkler's final telephone call.

Among the items found on Hinkler's body was a letter that had been opened. This bore the date 12 December 1932 and began with the words, "My darling beloved." The writer could only have been Katherine and the date the letter bears indicates that, in the period of Hinkler's final delay, it was necessary for her to contact him by correspondence. In earlier years Hinkler had maintained a town address at Chichele Road, Cricklewood, but this arrangement apparently lapsed when he was in the U.S.A.

At the Great West Aerodrome on 7 January, after the evening meal with caretaker Harris and his wife, Bert Hinkler made two telephone calls. The last of these was to Glasgow Western 5560. The natural assumption is that he reserved his most important phone call until last. A check of the 1933 Glasgow telephone book for this number* produced the name W. B. Rome. This was Capt. William Brown Rome, said to be a Canadian sea captain. His son, William Wallace Rome, resided with him at 17 Falkland Mansions in Glasgow. They moved soon after to a nearby address, and this was reflected by a change in the telephone number. Local residents remembered that Captain Rome returned to the other side of the Atlantic about 1937 and that his son, who had been attending Glasgow Academy, left his sleigh or bicycle with a neighbour with whom he was friendly. Other than the coincidence that Hinkler was in Canada at various times between 1930 and 1932 and had

---

*A progressive check, entry by entry, from A onwards, to find the number and from this to establish the name. Search performed by L. A. Cordingley.

served with Canadians in World War I, there seems nothing to link Hinkler with Captain Rome personally. However, the residence to which the phone was connected, 17 Falkland Mansions, is the same address shown for Katherine Hinkler in the court records relating to the grant of letters of administration for Hinkler's estate. It was therefore Katherine to whom Bert Hinkler spoke in the last telephone call, some six hours before he took off from the Great West Aerodrome.

Katherine also had a nephew named Willie, and he was of an age that corresponded with that of Captain Rome's son, William. It seems possible that William W. Rome may have been Katherine's nephew. Be that as it may, from that telephone call onwards, throughout 1933, L. V. Pearkes and Katherine Hinkler participated in a continuing series of events. Their real attitude to Hinkler can be measured by awarding a score for the way they handled each event. The function of allocating specific scores will be left to the reader.

Event one, 8 January 1933, relates to the urgency, or otherwise, with which they endeavoured to have the missing aviator located and assisted. As of Sunday morning, 8 January, the search was on for someone who could speak with authority on Hinkler's intentions. A strange silence descended. In England that silence remained until the afternoon of Tuesday, 10 January, when the petrol company Shell Mex released the details of Hinkler's route. The *Daily Herald* that same morning had carried the report concerning the mystery woman whom Hinkler expected would look after his interests in the event of anything untoward occurring to him, the woman who had subsequently done nothing.

The same *Daily Herald* coverage of Hinkler's disappearance also asserted, on the basis of widespread press enquiries, that no other person in England had been left in charge of Hinkler's affairs. In some Australian newspapers that same morning of 10 January, a significant and apparently contradictory report appeared. Because of the time zone difference this report was actually published ten hours before the *Daily Herald* appeared on the streets of London. Though it contradicted the *Daily Herald* and other British newspapers, it cited no source for its information. It said that Hinkler appointed "a firm of solicitors" as his business agents "on the eve of his departure." There are two issues raised by this claim: the first is its authenticity; the second is its consequences. It is the second aspect that comes under scrutiny at this point; the authenticity of the claim will be examined later.

During the period when it was still possible for Hinkler to have reappeared or to have been found alive, the "woman friend" mentioned in the newspaper article never came forward. If that woman is to be considered as different from Katherine, then it is necessary to add that Katherine Hinkler never came forward either. The "firm of solicitors" did nothing to initiate or promote or support any attempt at a search effort. So little information was available in England that the Air Ministry found it necessary to seek assistance from the B.B.C. and broadcasting organisations in Europe and the Balkans. Silence continued. Pearkes—when the "firm of solicitors" mask was dropped—later criticised the "unofficial" search effort that was launched by a well-meaning committee of Hinkler's friends in the first days of Hinkler's disappearance, but he did nothing himself.

On this issue, their failure to seek or promote a search effort, Pearkes and Katherine are scoring well but on the wrong side of the ledger.

Event number two: By the end of January 1933 it was certain Hinkler was dead. His friends organised a memorial service at the City Temple for 5 February. At this date Bert Hinkler would have been missing for twenty-nine days. The arrangement was peremptorily squashed by Pearkes, now identified as an individual rather than a "firm," speaking in an authoritative manner totally lacking when there was some chance Hinkler would reappear. His language was conspicuously not that of conciliation and moderation. It should have been, for the search committee members had acted out of respect for Hinkler. Cancellation of the service by Pearkes effectively concealed the existence of Katherine Hinkler by eliminating the need for any public appearance on her part, even incognito. Forgetful of having blocked the memorial service, both Pearkes and Katherine were later critical of the absence of any indication of regard in England for the missing aviator.

The pattern of scoring seems to be well in place by this time.

Event numbers three and four: At the end of January the first report from the French inspector of forests and waterways, M. P. Saby, reached England. It seemed fairly clear that the aircraft that

Saby heard flying overhead at Sens was Hinkler's Puss Moth. Pearkes subsequently showed considerable interest in Saby's activities, examining his report with the secretary of the Royal Aero Club and representing to the French air attaché that continuation of Saby's investigations could produce a fruitful result.

Unfortunately, the reason for the solicitor's interest was so that he could make "an early Application to the Court" for presumption of Hinkler's death and proceed to the finalisation of his affairs. That reason was stated not by a critic of the solicitor but by the solicitor himself.

Had Saby's search been successful and the wrecked aircraft found, the connection established by the solicitor direct with the Frenchman would have proved most advantageous. Pearkes would have been able to establish immediate control over the body and personal effects. What that would have meant is spelt out by the event itself, event four, when it did occur in Italy. The intention was to bury the body quietly, quickly, and permanently. At the state funeral in Florence, with a touch of irony that is historic, the solicitor was cast in the role of the "Principal Mourner."

Event number five: During his stay in Italy Pearkes showed an immediate and anxious interest in a document that had been specifically referred to in the first press reports of the crash. He certainly could not be accused of lassitude in his pursuit of it—the passport issued to Hinkler at Ottawa in Canada on 18 March 1932. At the point in time when the passport was issued, Hinkler intended to return to England in April. He was delayed somewhat by a marriage that took place on 21 May 1932. The endorsements in the passport were either at variance with, or revelatory of, the legal situation as it existed from 21 May onwards—a subject to be kept from prying eyes, particularly with reburial as an issue of continuing interest to the Australian government and the press and with the application to the Probate Court coming up.

Corollary event (to the legal widow's inheritance of Hinkler's estate): Bert Hinkler's estate in England and Australia amounted to over £12,000, a fairly considerable sum indeed. Some months after letters of administration were granted to the legal widow, the Australian government waived the necessity for Hinkler's mother to make an application for a pension and granted her an annuity. In the correspondence that gave rise to this decision, the word "indigent" was used in respect to Mrs. Frances Hinkler.

Event number six: Then came the Italian tribute—a memorial on the crest of the mountain overlooking the crash site—produced with genuine class, style, and artistry on the part of the workmen and designer. A handwritten card bearing her name accompanied the wreath from the widow. It was held by Katherine to be a particular virtue of the solicitor that he once again stood in for her at the ceremony. Throughout eight months of 1933 Pearkes had shown attention above and beyond the call of duty to the wishes of the vivacious and attractive Katherine, even, it would seem, to the neglect of other legal duties. He had shown less than no interest in attending the memorial service in London on behalf of "the widow" at the end of January.

If the score for the Italian memorial episode be regarded at best as "neutral," on the grounds that the options were restricted, it nevertheless represents a continuation of the very same modus operandi that characterised what might be described as the compact between the solicitor and the widow throughout 1933. The guidelines and themes that they pursued were the same at the end of the year as they were at the beginning.

All the scores are on the wrong side of the ledger. But Bert Hinkler, in a sense, did exact retribution from the grave. There was an additional factor of which Katherine Hinkler had every reason to be well aware and undoubtedly Pearkes, too. It squares the ledger a little and no doubt magnified their behind-the-scenes contortions, giving their performances a Laurel and Hardy touch. On 21 May 1932, when the marriage took place, the man who married Katherine was undoubtedly Herbert John Louis Hinkler of Bundaberg, Queensland, and just as unquestionably that was the name that Katherine knew him by. It is not, however, the name that appears on the marriage license and it is not the name in which the marriage was solemnised before a justice of the peace.

Peculiarly, the surname shown in the passport found on Hinkler's body had been obliterated "by the weather." Did the solicitor see something in this curious circumstance that gave him cause for anxiety?*

It appears that no official or person in authority asked for the production of the marriage certificate or checked the claim of marriage back to its source. Exactly what would have occurred had any such request been made can only be conjectured. Legal authorities attest that it was not necessary to support the application to the Probate Court by production of evidence of the marriage.

Taking the score card into account in relation to the point in time at which the compact between Katherine and Pearkes began to operate, it is reasonable to conclude not only that the compact did not come into existence for any beneficial effect it might have upon Bert Hinkler, but that it actually betrays an expectancy—foreknowledge—on the part of both Katherine and Pearkes of the probability that Hinkler would lose his life on the flight he was about to undertake. It is with this in mind that an examination must begin of the authenticity of the solicitor's claim to have been appointed by the missing airman. But first there is another matter that must be scored—the ransacking of the Thornhill home.

*Hinkler's marriage under a different name has numerous levels of significance. The implications of the passport incident are also considerable. Was the obliterated name *Hinkler*? Or was it the name shown on the marriage license? If the latter, as almost certainly it would have been, was it Hinkler himself who effaced the surname before the flight? Have we not here the clearest possible signal of a dramatic change in Hinkler's perception of the marriage? Was the expunging of the name totally effective or would the name have become apparent under close examination? (Canadian government records relating to the issue of the passport have been destroyed.)

# Two Air Powers Join Hinkler Hunt

## NOT A WORD SINCE SATURDAY

### WIFE REFUSES TO GIVE UP HOPE

By Our Air Correspondent

THE air forces of two great Powers, Italy and France, joined last night in a search for Squadron-Leader Bert Hinkler, the Australian flyer.

Up to an early hour this morning the Air Ministry had received no word from Hinkler since he left Feltham Aerodrome, Middlesex, on Saturday morning.

He was bound for Brindisi, Southern Italy, on the first stage of a record-breaking flight to Australia.

The Italian Air Ministry, at the request of the "Daily Herald" last night, issued instructions to all air force stations throughout Italy to search for Hinkler.

A telephone call to the Paris Air Ministry from the "Daily Herald" also resulted in a promise that the French air services would co-operate with the Italian aviators in the search for the world-famous flyer.

An amazing position arose in England yesterday. There was no one in this country who was prepared to take the responsibility of inaugurating a search for Hinkler and his plane.

Hinkler made the flight purely as a personal venture; he had no

financial backers; he was using his own machine; and he had not arranged with anyone to look after his affairs.

Mrs. Hinkler, the airman's wife, left England recently and is now in Australia, awaiting her husband's arrival. She said, last night, that she was not unduly worried.

IF ANYTHING HAPPENED . . . .

"My husband always turns up some time or other," she added.

"I am able to reveal that Hinkler had made private arrangements with a woman friend, of himself and his wife, that if anything serious arose he would telegraph her.

This woman friend had been told to get in touch with Mr. F. Hazell Jones, an aviation expert in London. Hinkler, before he left, entirely forgot, however, to complete the final arrangements of this one and only English contact.

Last night, Mr. Jones told me that he was very perturbed about Hinkler's disappearance.

"I am not acting for him in any way, officially," he added. "He told me would be cabled if anything urgent arose, but he did not tell me who she was."

"Daily Herald." I communicated with the Italian Air Ministry. General Balbo's chief assistant told me the Ministry had no official intimation that Hinkler was flying over Italy.

"If there is any chance that he is lost in our country," he declared, "we will certainly search for him The Italian Air Force will be warned immediately to make every effort to find your airman."

Daily Herald (UK) 10.1.33

Mrs. Hinkler

# MR. HINKLER
## STILL MISSING.
### Air Search in Italy.

LONDON, Jan. 10.

There is still no news of Mr. Bert Hinkler, who has been missing since he left London last Saturday on a flight to Australia. His 83 hours' silence disposes of the theory that he landed at a remote aerodrome, refuelled, and went on, because he would since have had to alight for further fuel somewhere in Asia, and reports from there indicate that no trace of him has been found.

The Italian Air Ministry has issued instructions to all air stations to search for Mr. Hinkler. The French air service is co-operating.

The Italian Air Ministry says that if Mr. Hinkler crashed in the Alps he may not be heard of for a long time. An Italian pilot who was recently forced down in the Alps was not traced for two months.

The "Daily Herald," which put the facts before Italian and French Ministries, emphasises the "amazing position when no one in England is prepared to take the responsibility of inaugurating a search, as Mr. Hinkler has no financial backers and is using his own machine."

An Italian Air Ministry official said that Mr. Hinkler had not landed at any emergency aerodrome in Italy

"We have no record of his applying for a permit to fly over Italy," he added. "The British Air Ministry has not requested a search."

The British Air Ministry is of the opinion that Mr. Hinkler did not need a permit, because Italy is a member of the International Convention. An official said that owing to Mr. Hinkler's secrecy they did not know his route. Consequently it was difficult to ask anyone to search for him.

Mr. Hinkler made a private arrangement with a woman friend that if anything serious arose he would telegraph her, the friend being told to get into touch with Mr. Hazel Jones, a London aviation expert; but Mr. Hinkler even forgot to complete this arrangement, as he did not tell Mr. Jones the woman's name.

Sydney Morning Herald 11.1.33

---

Hobart Mercury 11.1.33

WEDNESDAY, JANUARY 11, 1933

# HINKLER STILL MISSING

### AMAZING POSITION
### NO ONE RESPONSIBLE.

The "Daily Herald," which put the facts before the Italian and French Ministries yesterday, emphasised the "amazing position," when no one in England is prepared to take the responsibility of inaugurating a search, as Hinkler had no financial backing, and was using his own machine.

INCOMPLETE ARRANGEMENT.

He made a private arrangement with a woman friend, said the journal, that if

way, and why is unknown, he declares Mr. G. W. A. Scott. "Hinkler, unlike he did on his record flight in 1928, may have flown by way of North Africa, in order to avoid the mountains between Brindisi and Athens, and possibly has been forced down on a lonely part of the coast."

IF CRASHED ON THE ALPS.

ROME, January 10.

Hinkler has crashed on the Alps he may not be heard of for a long time. An Italian pilot was recently forced down on the Alps, and was not traced for two months.

TASMAN ___

STA

A Decin

# The Ransacked House

Bert Hinkler's mother,
Frances Atkins Hinkler.

The Home of Bert and Nancy at Thornhill on the outskirts of Southampton, 1930.

# 11

# EIGHT GALLONS OF PETROL

On hearing of the discovery of Bert Hinkler's body, his brother George made a significant comment as to the way Bert Hinkler viewed the world: "Bert was always his mother's boy. Despite his crowded life of adventure, he always found time regularly to write to her."

Earlier, in 1928, Bert's mother had stated her viewpoint: "Bert and I were more like pals than mother and son. When he went down the street he would buy little things for me, and I would do the same for him. When he broke the wheels of his glider after trying it out on Sandhills Beach, I scraped together two guineas to buy him a new pair from Melbourne. I never repressed or deceived my children, and they have always been happy and dutiful. Bert never had a penny of assistance from anybody all his life. He won through with his own hard work and determination."

There was nothing effeminate or unmanly about Hinkler. His record speaks for itself. No man showed more courage or fortitude in war or peace. Yet his concern for his mother was a most significant element in the structure of his thought processes. When Hinkler made the pioneering solo flight from England to Australia in 1928 and became the pacesetter for much of what took place over the route in the next seven years, he was spoken of as "monarch of the air" and the flight itself characterised by some commentators as "a flight home to mother." Indeed it was, and Hinkler was pleased to give his mother some reason to be proud of her son and her family. He was not indifferent to the reaction of the Australian or British public, far from it, but he did not exhibit his special talent on the world stage for the purpose of gaining public approbation. The form of such approbation often took him genuinely by surprise. There was always a purpose behind Hinkler's achievements and that purpose was connected to bringing to fulfillment the potential of aviation as he saw it, not in any abstract sense, but in a particular way answering to a design that had formed in his mind. If public applause recognised the true nature and value of the achievement, if the results in some way enabled him to continue pursuing the course of his own destiny, solo as in the past, then Bert Hinkler asked for no more.

Hinkler's life was a life of endeavour and on that stage his mother was his permanent audience. The strong bond between mother and son was not the result of any intellectual decision but came as naturally and as unquestioned to Hinkler as the impulse to fly with which he was also born.

Any appraisal of events surrounding Bert Hinkler's last flight that takes into account the previously unacknowledged existence of Katherine Hinkler must begin from the receipt by Hinkler's mother in Bundaberg in 1932 of the news from Hinkler of his relationship with Katherine and what that implied in respect to Nancy. It is unlikely Hinkler went so far as to inform his mother, at this stage, of what had taken place on 21 May 1932; he clearly did not. His mother seemed not to know anything at all of that matter until at least June 1933; and then only after consulting a lawyer. While ever the bond between mother and son lasted, there would always be order in Hinkler's world, even during the chaos of a world at war. The bond remained but Hinkler's feeling of order dissolved when he received his mother's opinion of the news he sent in his letter.

A letter can be an unintentionally brutal way of conveying information or of expressing an opinion. No doubt Frances Hinkler opened the letter from her son with the usual feeling of pleasure she experienced on such occasions. The news of Katherine's involvement with her son took her completely by surprise and her reply was a spontaneous reaction, perhaps too unrestrained and too soon expressed. Frances Hinkler was not lost for words and her comments no doubt included a summing up of her opinion of the younger woman with whom Bert had allowed himself to become involved. Hinkler's sister-in-law in Bundaberg and his brother Jack remembered that time of sorrow well and the reaction of Hinkler's mother. They knew better than most that Bert's action—he was aged thirty-nine and had spent a lifetime with flying machines—may well have arisen out of concern for a living memorial of flesh and blood. But when Bert received his mother's reply it clearly had a shattering effect upon him, possibly more so because it would have reinforced any unease he already felt.

C. G. Grey, editor of *Aeroplane* magazine, had a private discussion with Hinkler just before Hinkler left on the final flight. Something had left Hinkler's life. Grey later put his impressions of that meeting into print:

> We have lost an extraordinarily good man in Bert Hinkler, but we need not sympathise with him or even mourn for him. I had a long talk with him the day before he intended to start on his last journey. He was as keen on success as ever, but he did not care what happened to himself. . . . He was as cheerful and as amusing and as good company as ever, but he had got to the state when he did not care very much about anything. He was far too brave, and far too deeply religious in the full sense of the word, to commit suicide, but he just did not care. If he got through all would be well, and if he did not, there would be an end of it. . . .

After Hinkler had been missing for a week, his home at Thornhill was ransacked. The house was entered at some time between 1:45 P.M. Sunday, 15 January, and 8:00 A.M. Monday, 16 January. This pinpointing of the period indicates the break-in took place on the Sunday night. Hinkler's nearest neighbour was a farmer named Stride, whose house was at some distance. Details appeared in the *Southampton Daily Echo* on Tuesday, 17 January:

## HINKLER'S HOUSE BROKEN INTO
## EVERY ROOM FOUND IN STATE OF DISORDER

Southampton police are investigating a robbery which occurred during the week-end at Mon Repos, Thornhill Park, Sholing, the home of Squadron Leader "Bert" Hinkler, the famous airman. . . .

The house is situated in a rather isolated spot on the edge of the borough boundary and is hidden from the main road by a thick belt of trees. When Mr. Fred Hailey, a postman, of 53, Merry Oak-road, Southampton, called at the house yesterday morning he found signs that it had been forcibly entered. He at once reported the matter to the police. It was discovered that entry had been gained by smashing a pane of glass in the dining room window near the catch.

HOUSE RANSACKED

On entering the house the police found every room in a state of disorder. Drawers and cupboards were open and their contents, in some cases, were strewn about the floor. At present it is impossible to say what has been taken as Mrs. Hinkler, the airman's wife, is in New Zealand, and the house has been unoccupied for several weeks. The intruders apparently left the house by the back door, which leads into a conservatory. The conservatory door was found to be unlocked. . . .

The Brisbane *Daily Mail* included much of the above in its report, but it also included a matter of specific local interest:

# MOTHER'S PORTRAITS DAMAGED

The police are asking Hinkler's friends whether souvenirs, gifts and trophies were removed. Hinkler's home was left in pathetic disorder. The contents of drawers and cupboards were strewn about the floor and photographs of the airman's mother, brought from Bundaberg in Queensland, had been knocked off the wall and the face trodden in. . . .

The *Sydney Morning Herald* of 19 January gave a little space to the item, which it received through the Australian Press Association, but added the information: "An adjoining shed in which Mr. Hinkler kept his self-designed Ibis amphibian was entered, but the machine was not damaged."

A second report, which appeared in the Southampton *South-*

*ern Daily Echo* of Wednesday, 18 January, dealt with the aftermath:

# ONLY PETROL MISSING?

So far as the Southampton police are able to ascertain at present, the only articles missing from Mon Repos, Thornhill Park, Sholing, the home of Squadron Leader Bert Hinkler, which was broken into during the weekend, are four two-gallon tins of petrol which were in the garage. . . . A friend who was left with the key of the house went over the house with the police yesterday. . . . The friend believes that the only thing stolen were the tins of petrol which were in the garage, the door of which had been forced.

Some of the characteristics and interests of the ransackers can be established from the data provided by their activity. The Hinkler home was a short distance from the Southampton to Portsmouth Road, in an isolated area. It was hidden by trees. No other house in the nearby area reported a break-in. The ransacking occurred on a Sunday night. Hinkler's house was the specific target of a planned operation. The intruders knew in advance the house was unoccupied and that their entry would not be challenged. They arrived by car. All that appeared to be missing were eight gallons of petrol in four separate cans. The ransackers had come a long distance and faced difficulty refuelling for the return journey on a Sunday night. Eight gallons was more than ample for a journey from Southampton to London, even by the longer route thrugh Portsmouth and the coastal resorts. The only consequence the intruders were concerned with was to locate documents. They were not concerned to conceal their presence. They carried out their enterprise with speed. There was no indication, from the thoroughness of the search, that they found what they were look-ing for. They were not common thieves. At least one photograph of Bert Hinkler's mother was thrown on the floor and the face trodden in. An intruder either had taken an instant dislike to Mrs. Frances Hinkler's face or bore some animosity towards her that existed before the ransacking. This implies that the intruder had some personal knowledge of Bert Hinkler's mother.

Where, then, in England, on the night of Sunday, 15 January 1933, would we look for a person or persons who had such an anxious interest in personal documents belonging to Bert Hinkler?

The police who investigated the break-in were unable to identify those responsible.

It is indeed a strange coincidence that, unknown to the public, there were in England at that time two persons who had a direct interest in Hinkler's affairs. One was L.V. Pearkes, the other was Katherine Hinkler. Pearkes, who was allegedly appointed by Hinkler just before the aviator departed, had allowed Hinkler to leave on a dangerous flight without obtaining even the simplest form of will from him. If Hinkler was found to have died intestate, it might make the story of Pearkes's appointment look a little thin. Katherine, of course, had an obvious vested interest in the contents of a will. She also had a vested interest in any documents that might have been left lying about in the house that could result in her being prematurely identified or, alternatively, identified as the woman referred to in the *Daily Herald* article published some five days previously. Bert Hinkler had flown to Hamble on his final day in England and that was only a short distance away: perhaps he called at the house while in the area. If so, to what purpose? Could he have left a message there for Nancy to find on her return?

The interests of the intruders, as far as they can be established, coincided with the interests of Pearkes and Katherine Hinkler. This is self-evident. It goes without saying that no movie film exists of the ransacking actually taking place. If there were such a film, would it not be enlightening to watch the expression on the face of the intruder who was grinding a heel into the face of Bert Hinkler's mother?

And if we suppose for a moment that the intruder's face is that of Katherine, what would it tell us about the impact made upon Bert Hinkler by his mother's letter, and of the secret springs of thought and action of the great airman himself when measured by the criterion enunciated by his brother George? Supposing, for a moment, that a movie film of the ransacking by the intruders, whoever they were, did exist, what effect might it have upon the "score card" for Katherine Hinkler and L. V. Pearkes? A plus? Neutral? Minus? The one certainty is that it does not create any credit points for either of them and holds out the possibility of a very big minus.

There might be a temptation, because of the special circumstances, to start a score card of a different kind for Mrs. Frances Hinkler, Bert's mother. That temptation becomes easier to resist when it is remembered that within a few hours of Hinkler's disappearance, it was his mother who raised the question that the aircraft had been tampered with.

# ..rn Daily Echo

## .Y THROUGHOUT HANTS, WILTS, DORSET, and the ISLE OF WIGHT.

SOUTHAMPTON, TUESDAY, JANUARY 17, 1933.

TELEPHONE N.
.5 Lines.

# .THOUT MAKING A STAT

## OFF TO WARMER CLIMES.

"Echo" photo.

Details for service overseas on the troopship Nevasa, which left Southampton to-day.

## MR. LLOYD GEORGE 70 TO-DAY.

### Messages from Friends and Foes.

### "SOUND" PICTURE WITH HIS FAMILY.

CRICCIETH, Tuesday.

M R. LLOYD GEORGE, who was 70 to-day, was smothered with congratulations. He was embraced by his children and his grand-children.

New Year's Honours list. Their friendship has passed through many vicissitudes. They have worked together and drifted apart politically, and have been re-united, but at the present moment they are political opponents. Their personal esteem

## HINKLER'S HOUSE BROKEN INTO

### Every Room Found in State of Disorder.

S OUTHAMPTON police are investigating a robbery which occurred during the week-end at Mon Repos, Thornhill Park, Sholing, the home of Squadron Leader "Bert" Hinkler, the famous airman, of whom no news has been received since he set out from England on his attempt to fly to Australia in record time more than ten days ago.

The house is situated in a rather isolated spot on the edge of the borough boundary and is hidden from the main road by a thick belt of trees. When Mr. Fred Hailey, a postman, of 53, Merry Oak-road, Southampton, called at the house yesterday morning he found signs that it had been forcibly entered. He at once reported the matter to the police.

It was discovered that entry had been gained by smashing a pane of glass in the dining room window near the catch.

On entering the house the police found every room in a state of disorder. Drawers and cupboards were open and their contents, in some cases, were strewn about the floor.

At present it is impossible to say what has been taken, as Mrs. Hinkler, the airman's wife, is in New Zealand, and the house has been unoccupied for several weeks.

The intruders apparently left the house by the back door, which leads into a conservatory. The conservatory door was found to be unlocked.

In addition, the door of a garage had been forced and a window of a shed in the garden, in which is kept the Squadron-Leader's small amphibian monoplane, was smashed.

The 'plane was apparently undamaged. The robbery was committed between 1.45 p.m. on Sunday and 8 a.m. yesterday.

+ - - - - - - - - - - - - +
## TEST MATCH

"Echo" Special Editions
+ - - - - - - - - - - - - +

## HAMPS.

## OF

### *But Be$*
### *S*

## "PASSIN

" T HE past season h. most successful but, financially, working has ag in a heavy loss."

This statement is m. annual report for 1932, ju the Hampshire County C.

"The committee," the tinues, "sincerely regret off in the membership and appeals to all existi. not only to continue th. but to do their utmost to members. Subscriptions by 1,983 members, 406 l. and 105 juniors."

### Players Accept
### Reductions.

"In spite of many econ. has been a loss on the a. working of £1,070 15s. 9. pleasing to record that realising the serious cr. which the club is pa. accepted reductions in the tions for 1933."

It is noted that the. menced with an overdra. 0s. 5d. This has been £2,809 18s. 6d., by mea. ment of a loan of £900 fr. County Cricket Ground C. an advance from them c. further special effort. £1,228 15s. 11d.

There was, as stated, a normal year's working of 9d., but, after bring. "exceptional receipts," surplus of £158 0s. 2d. o.. The loss is attribute. "resignations and death. and the extremely weather experienced at .l during the July Festival.

### Praise For
### Players.

Dealing with the playe.

# THE BLANDEST REPORT OF ALL TIME

Sydney Morning Herald 10.1.33

## MR. HINKLER.

### Still Missing.

#### ANXIETY INCREASING.

LONDON, Jan. 8.

No news has been received of the Australian airman, Mr. Bert Hinkler, since he left London early on Saturday morning on a flight to Australia.

On the eve of his departure Mr. Hinkler appointed a firm of solicitors as his business agents, and they had had no news of him at 2 o'clock this afternoon, which discounts the prevalent theory that he refuelled at an out-of-the-way place and began his second hop without being recognised. This also is minimised by the fact that the Australian Press Association has definitely established that Athens was to be Hinkler's first fuelling call.

---

*Hinkler's Body Found*

## ONLY ONE MAN KNEW HIS ROUTE

A pneumatic boat with oars was found in the cabin of the machine. There were several Canadian Government bonds and some Italian silver money on the body.

It was on January 7 that Hinkler set out in his Puss Moth monoplane, to smash all records for the flight to Australia.

He clothed all his plans in the deepest secrecy, and only three friends were on the Great West Aerodrome, Middlesex, to see him go.

Those three friends were the last people to see Hinkler alive.

Captain W. L. Hope searched for him by air in the Alps, but could find no one who had seen the machine.

After making some of the finest long-distance flights, Hinkler was a disappointed man, and, so bitter was he against the lack of appreciation shown him that he determined to let no one know of his plans for the Australian flight.

Only a few people knew whether he was flying to Australia or the Cape, and only one man, the official of a big petrol company, knew the actual route he was taking.

Hinkler was trying to reach Australia in seven days.

His wife had gone to Australia ahead of him and until the last, she was convinced that her husband was still alive.

## THREE-LEGGED CAT WAITS IN VAIN

Hinkler's three-legged cat has been patiently awaiting her master's return since he set out on his last flight. The cat is being tended by Mr. Elride, a farmer of Sholing, a village on the outskirts of Southampton.

"When Bert is on a long-distance flight he always likes to make the first hop a good one, and also prefers to fly high. I think it is quite possible that he may have been flying high with a following wind, and thus he might have passed over Brindisi without being seen. No news does not necessarily mean bad news. I am proud of my husband's flying, and have implicit faith in his ability."

Mrs Hinkler says that the date of her departure for Sydney depends on further news of her husband.

---

It was a stray, found with a hind leg caught in a steel trap in a field near Hinkler's home. The leg was broken, but Hinkler nursed the cat and made a cork leg for it.

Sholing looked upon the cat as Hinkler's mascot.

[Editorial on Page Ten]

---

Melbourne Argus 10.1.33

## HINKLER'S FLIGHT.

### GROWING ANXIETY.

#### AIRMEN OPTIMISTIC.

### May Have Landed in Balkans.

LONDON, Jan. 9.

It is more than 48 hours since Squadron-Leader Hinkler left Feltham aerodrome on a record-breaking flight to Australia, and much anxiety is being felt for his safety. Italy has not yet received a request to organise a search, as his friends suggest that the weather may have caused him to change his plans en route, and he may have decided to fly to Constantinople via Central Europe.

British newspapers are reflecting the general anxiety, but airmen suggest that if he descended in an inaccessible spot in the Balkans ... [text cut off] ...

... may have gone down to North Africa to avoid the mountains between Brindisi and Athens. Possibly he has been forced down on a lonely part of the coast."

Later.

On the eve of his departure Hinkler appointed a firm of solicitors as his business agents. They had no news of him at 2 o'clock this afternoon, which discounts the prevalent theory that, unrecognised, he refuelled at some out-of-the-way place and began a record hop. This is also minimised by the fact that the Australian Press Association has definitely established that Athens was Hinkler's first fuelling call.

It is now feared that Hinkler encountered trouble over the Adriatic or over one of the myriad islands off the Greek coast. Even the most sanguine of Hinkler's friends is becoming anxious since inquiry at every large centre as far as Cairo has been fruitless.

Another theory is that he was forced down in the Alps, but experts say that with the load he carried Hinkler could not have obtained sufficient altitude to cross the Alps, and he would therefore take the flatter route past Marseilles.

### Wife Not Unduly Alarmed.

AUCKLAND (N.Z.), Monday.—Although she is naturally concerned at the lack of news of her husband, Mrs. Hinkler, who is at present in Auckland, is not unduly alarmed. "When Bert is making a long-distance flight he always likes to make the first hop a good one," she said to-day, "and he also prefers to fly high. I think it is possible that he may have been flying high with a following wind, and thus has passed over Brindisi without being seen."

---

Brisbane Courier 10.1.33

# STOP PRESS

### FEARS GROWING.

#### NO NEWS OF HINKLER.

##### TROUBLE IN ADRIATIC!

LONDON, January 9.

On the eve of his departure Squadron-Leader Hinkler appointed a firm of solicitors as his business agents. They had no news of him at 2 p.m., which discounts the prevalent theory that he had not been recognised, and refuelled in an out of the way place, and began the second hop. This also is minimised by the fact that the Australian Press Association has definitely established that Athens was Hinkler's first call for fuelling.

It is now feared that Hinkler encountered trouble in the Adriatic, or on one of the myriad islands of the Grecian coast. Even his most sanguine friends are becoming anxious since inquiry at every large centre as far as Cairo, has proved fruitless. Another theory is that he has been forced down in the Alps, but experts say that with the load Hinkler carried on his machine the altitude would obtain would be insufficient to allow him to cross the Alps. He would, therefore, take the less mountainous route past Marseilles.

---

*Daily Herald (UK) 29.4.33*

... who goes ... Worry is ... A. Scott, Australia

---

# 12

# ON THE EVE OF HIS DEPARTURE

The assertion that Bert Hinkler appointed a "firm of solicitors" on the eve of his departure first appeared in a message transmitted from London to Australian newspapers. It was sent by an Australian news service at 2:00 P.M. London time on Monday, 9 January 1933. As published in the *Sydney Morning Herald* of 10 January, it read: "On the eve of his departure Hinkler appointed a firm of solicitors as his business agents. They had no news of him at 2 o'clock. . . ."

The report cited no source. Despite the extensive enquiries being made in England for someone to come forward and speak with authority on Hinkler's behalf, this piece of information was completely unknown to the London press, so much so that the *Daily Herald*, in its issue of 10 January, said that no one had been left in charge of Hinkler's affairs. Because of the time-zone factor the *Daily Herald* was actually reporting a situation existing ten hours later than the Australian press report of the same date, and this accentuates the disparity.

The assertion arose some fifty-nine hours after Hinkler departed and at a time when he was already forty hours or more overdue at his first stopping place. Bert Hinkler, wherever he was, was in no position to refute the claim. The newspaper report referred not to a single solicitor but to a corporate body, a "firm of solicitors," and indicated that this firm was to act as Hinkler's "business agents." There are several strange features about this alleged appointment. First, why would Hinkler leave it until 6 January 1933 to make such an arrangement when he had originally hoped to leave for Australia on 14 October 1932 and had already endured a series of frustrating delays until he took off some eighty-five days later on 7 January 1933? Second, why would he

111

appoint "business agents" in connection with his flight, when there was no possibility whatever of there being any business to conduct and where every hour of the flight added to the distance between the airman and his alleged agent? Third, why is there no documentary evidence whatever that Hinkler ever carried out such an appointment? Fourth, how and when did Hinkler get time on that last day in England to make this arrangement? It runs counter to the purpose of his known activities, which were primarily farewell visits. Fifth, why is it that every available record, both of correspondence and of telephone calls, shows Hinkler to be in action himself, handling all his affairs in his customary manner? Sixth, and most specifically, how did it come about that Hinkler died intestate, when the making of the simplest form of will and the naming of an executor would have been foremost in the mind of a business agent who was also a solicitor, particularly having regard to the dangers of the flight on which Hinkler was about to embark?

These considerations at once bring the claim under considerable suspicion. Furthermore, the conduct attributed to Hinkler was foreign to his lifelong attitudes. Should Hinkler not have survived, the claim effectively gave control of his affairs to the solicitor.

On the day following Hinkler's departure a peculiar situation had arisen in England. It would have been reasonable to expect the Air Ministry, on becoming aware that Hinkler had failed to make good his first intended landing place, to issue an announcement indicating the route that the missing airman was following. Such an announcement was not forthcoming, and in fact the Air Ministry said it was not aware of Hinkler's intentions. Shell Mex, the petrol company that laid down supplies along Hinkler's route to Australia, also refused to release information in its possession because of a request by Hinkler, when making arrangements, for confidentiality. This situation created the need for anyone claiming to represent Hinkler to come forward immediately. It was in such circumstances that the claim emerged—in the Australian press— that a firm of solicitors could speak with Hinkler's authority, at least on "business" matters. A review of all the factors shows that this claim was made at this point in time simply because it had to be made; the circumstances forced it. We shall also see that precisely because it had to be made prematurely, it had to be made both anonymously and deviously.

In the early period of Hinkler's disappearance, the firm of solicitors—brought to public knowledge in its alleged role only because of an unusual set of events—is completely anonymous and there is an absence of any input by it into public efforts to have a search instituted. The "firm" displayed no interest in moving to succour the missing airman. This was the period in which Bert might still reappear. There is virtually no reference whatever—certainly no direct first-hand reference—in the British press to the role or even existence of the solicitors at this time.

The initial assertion was unequivocal: the authority of the firm of solicitors derived directly from Bert Hinkler, not from any other person. Yet the influence of the solicitor, and his supposed knowledge of Hinkler's intentions, so lacked authority that the Air Ministry acted as though he was nonexistent: the Ministry's request to the BBC and the subsequent telegram to broadcasting authorities in Europe, end any argument on this point before it can begin.*

Katherine had not been present at the Great West Aerodrome to bid farewell to Hinkler. When he departed on Saturday, 7 January, she was in Scotland. Offices in London were shut over the weekend. The reasonable expectation by Monday morning, 9 January, was that the Air Ministry and Shell Mex would announce details of Hinkler's flight. When it became evident on Monday that they were unable to do so, which was a totally unforeseeable development, only then would it have been obvious and logical for Katherine to take steps to make known to the Air Ministry what she knew of Hinkler's intentions. Instead, there is silence from her with a claim emerging at the same time through a comparatively obscure news agency that Hinkler had appointed a solicitor just before he left. From this it follows that the solicitor, should his claim be proved spurious, was no more than a front for Katherine from the outset and that the arrangement that existed at the time of Hinkler's departure was an arrangement initiated by Katherine in her own interests and in the light of her knowledge of what was about to occur.

*See page 16. The telegram was sent on Thursday, 12 January 1933.

It could not be claimed, at that time, that the solicitor's authority derived from Hinkler's "widow" because as yet she was not a widow, and, in fact, could hardly be considered such until about ten days had elapsed without word of the missing airman. Had the Air Ministry immediately released Hinkler's route, or had Bert Hinkler's crashed aircraft been reported at once, the problem would not have arisen for Katherine, for the first the public would have known of the solicitor would have been in his normal legal setting of finalising Hinkler's estate.

When the lapse of time made certain that Hinkler was dead, there was a sudden shift to a higher profile. The firm of solicitors became personalised in the form of L. V. Pearkes, and far from being silent and inert he was running swiftly and speaking authoritatively—very authoritatively indeed. At this time he could (if challenged) claim the support, if not the authority, of the "legal widow," and he felt on safer ground. All his activities had as their aim the furtherance of Katherine's interests.

When Hinkler's estate was finalised in June 1933, the solicitor did not present himself as the agent of the widow. She was the beneficiary. Pearkes did not act as Bert Hinkler's nominee either, but as the "intimate friend" of the deceased. This significantly altered the posture that had been asserted on 9 January. Katherine had her own solicitor, so she later informed others, and he had his offices at no. 2 Field Court, off Gray's Inn Place, London.

Because of intestacy provisions in respect to the Australian element in Hinkler's estate, no final acquittal of Hinkler's affairs could take place until the death of Katherine, an event that did not occur until over forty years later. Throughout those years, L. V. Pearkes was drawn somewhat out of his depth by a series of matters that arose concerning Hinkler. A strong element of contradiction emerged between his claim and his conduct. Eventually, after the death of Katherine, Pearkes was interviewed by the author. He produced various documents and a photograph of himself taken during World War I. He lent the latter item for reproduction in this book. In the presence of a third person Pearkes then stated:

• He had met Bert Hinkler when they served together in an RNAS squadron in World War I.
• He had not seen Bert Hinkler since World War I.

- When asked if he thought Bert Hinkler would have had a solicitor, he gave a short sudden laugh, adding a few words to indicate the incompatibility of such an idea with the Hinkler he knew.
- As a solicitor he did not approach the press in January 1933.
- He did not know who it was that gave his name to the press.

Thus, he was never appointed by Bert Hinkler and had not met him for at least fifteen years prior to the final flight.* The question was about to be put to him, Where and when did you first meet Katherine Hinkler? but there came an explosive utterance from a witness to the questioning who had heard a totally different story in the past, and unfortunately that little explosion effectively ended the questioning.

Without being aware of it, because he was unaware of the knowledge of the questioner on the point, the solicitor had admitted that on 7 January 1933 a compact existed between Katherine Hinkler and himself that was based entirely on their foreknowledge that Bert Hinkler would meet his death on the flight. The compact was arranged behind Bert's back.

One crucial question remained. A third person had given Pearkes's name to the press in 1933. There was no reason to doubt Pearkes when he said it was not himself and that he did not know who was responsible. Who was it? For whoever it was had been accepted as an authority by the Australian press service in London and his unique information was published without the source being revealed. This had enabled Pearkes to be accepted as having charge of Hinkler's affairs in circumstances where the cause of Hinkler's crash and death was very much open to the gravest suspicion. The identification of this third person is crucial.

One thing, however, had been established with reasonable certainty. In 1933 Pearkes was of athletic build, five feet nine inches in height, blue eyed, and fair haired. An intimate friend of Katherine's he may certainly have been, but he was definitely not an intimate friend of Bert Hinkler.

*Pearkes was thinking, and talking, about his own real experiences, about himself exclusively, not Hinkler. Being thus engrossed, unguarded the truth slipped out from him. This result was not accidental, as the interview had been structured with this possible consequence in view.

L. V. Pearkes at the inauguration ceremony.

The memorial inscription reads—
"Al transvolatore
    Herbert Hinkler
        qui caduto
            8-1-XI".

Year XI of the Fascist regime was 1933.

Photographs of the Memorial appeared in the London *Times* and the *Illustrated London News*.

## The 1933 Memorial

G. A. Lingham and Jack Savage

## 13

# HIS CLOSEST ASSOCIATES

In 1933 two main news agencies supplied news reports from London to Australian newspapers—the Australian Press Association and the Australian Cable Service. Individual newspapers subscribed to the service of their own choice. To cut costs the two services used a communal transmission for data that arose regularly in England and were transmitted daily. Reuters and an official wireless service were other sources drawn on by the Australian press. The Australian Press Association was responsible for the report that Hinkler appointed solicitors. It appeared in those newspapers in Australia that subscribed to the APA, sometimes with a delay because both the APA and the ACS communicated only with their own central offices in Australia, which then distributed the material to the other subscribing newspapers.

To meet the publishing deadlines of the morning press in Australia it was necessary for messages from the news services to be lodged in London by 2:00 P.M., equivalent to midnight in Australia. The message concerning the appointment of a "firm of solicitors," published in Australia on Tuesday morning, 10 January, was transmitted from London at 2:00 P.M. on Monday, 9 January. This means that the APA had received the information at a point in time no later than fifty-nine hours after Hinkler departed.

Where did the APA get this information from? On all sides it was being alleged that Hinkler had been extremely secretive. The Air Ministry said it knew nothing. The London press, despite extensive enquiries, were unable to locate any person, official or otherwise, who could speak on Hinkler's behalf. There were simply no sources of authentic information, other than possibly a small number of Hinkler's friends. As the assertion about Hinkler appointing the solicitor was spurious, the supplier of it had to remain anonymous or face Hinkler's wrath if he reappeared. The quite unexpected absence of an official authority able to speak on behalf of Hinkler meant that the assertion had to be made prematurely. The lack of certainty over Hinkler's fate meant it also had to be made deviously.

Had the claim reached the APA direct from Pearkes, he would have been asked for corroboration and the details (had they been genuine) would have made an interesting story. Pearkes, as his conduct demonstrated at various times, was a complete stranger to the 1933 aviation scene. Had the information come from Katherine Hinkler, it would have been an even more exciting contact for the reporter. Given the volume of effort that was expended in concealing the existence of Katherine, neither Pearkes nor Katherine were likely candidates for the role of press informant. They can be ruled out without any further consideration. If the information was received anonymously, it would have been under suspicion at once. The APA report, despite its brevity, contains three important clues concerning its originator: first, the person had to be in a position to know what Hinkler did on the eve of his departure; second, he had to be a person to whom Hinkler (despite his reputation for secrecy) might divulge a private arrangement; third, the informant had to be self-evidently acceptable to the reporter.

In the circumstances under which Hinkler prepared his machine and took off from England, these characteristics are virtually sufficient of themselves to point straight at the informant. But bearing each characteristic in mind, two lists can be prepared. The first is a list of the persons with whom Hinkler was known to have been in contact on the "eve of his departure." The second list is of those persons who might have been approached by either of the two Australian news agencies in London, the APA or the ACS, in their quest for information on Hinkler as early as 2:00 P.M. Monday, 9 January. Names common to both lists should include among them the one name that is the name of the informant. That one name should then be placed under close scrutiny.

To compile the first list it is necessary to work backwards

from Hinkler's actual takeoff. His two close acquaintances who assisted with the takeoff were Maj. Jack Savage and G. A. (Dopey) Lingham. Earlier the same evening, Hinkler had a chat at the dinner table with caretaker Harris and his wife. There were several telephone calls initiated by Hinkler—to Katherine Hinkler, Jack Savage, Joe Taylor of Shell Mex, and two to Croydon Airport. Prior to his arrival at the Great West Aerodrome, Hinkler had visited Customs at Croydon. Before that he had been at Hamble Aerodrome, where he'd landed the Puss Moth to attend a luncheon in his honour arranged by the Hampshire Aero Club. He also went into Southampton and visited his long-time friend Jim Laver. Earlier in the morning, before leaving Hendon for Hamble, Bert Hinkler had called upon two close friends from earlier days— L. H. Pike, the representative in London for the Queensland government, and C. G. Grey, editor of the magazine *Aeroplane*.

Jim Laver, Hinkler's closest friend, knew nothing of the alleged appointment. Pike could not under any circumstance have been the informant, and he knew nothing of it in any case. C. G. Grey of the *Aeroplane* is likewise ruled out. Given the sequence of events in which Shell Mex was involved prior to releasing the route, it would be absurd to suggest it was Joe Taylor of that company who contacted the press. Hinkler could hardly be expected to have divulged it to the staff he met casually at Fairey's aerodrome, including caretaker Harris and his wife, and it is certain he did not. Croydon Airport authorities would have contacted the Air Ministry, not a comparatively unknown Australian press agency. An account of the Hampshire Aero Club luncheon indicated Hinkler did not even divulge his intention of starting his flight the next morning.

The two possibilities that remain from the list of persons known to be in contact with Hinkler on the eve of his departure are Jack Savage and Dopey Lingham. Both these names were connected with the hangar in which Hinkler prepared his aircraft. The men were, in fact, long-time associates, though quite dissimilar in disposition to each other. Maj. Jack Savage, as he was known throughout the aviation industry in England, was not a pilot himself but had been involved with flying since 1910. He had developed a small business of his own and also become manager for a well-known exhibition flyer, Benny Hucks, the first British pilot to loop the loop. Jack Savage entered the Royal Naval Air Service in 1915, where he rose to the rank of lieutenant commander and received the MBE for his contribution to a wartime developmental programme connected with smoke screens and kite balloons. When the flying services amalgamated into the Royal Air Force in 1918, he became Maj. Jack Savage, the army rank being used at that time for the new service. The story of Jack Savage from 1922 onwards was the story of skywriting and sky projection, the former being performed by aeroplanes exuding smoke to spell letters and words and the latter being the projection of words onto clouds by means of a searchlight. The airman whose superlative flying introduced skywriting to the world from 1922 onwards was Cyril Turner. Savage built up around Turner a team of professionals who took skywriting to a score of countries. One of the pilots who joined him was Dopey Lingham, who had flown with 43 Squadron during the war.

Bert Hinkler was acquainted with Savage and Lingham at least as early as 1924. A Skywriting SE5 visited Hamble where Hinkler was chief test pilot for the Avro Company and later Hinkler demonstrated the effectiveness of an Avro oleo undercarriage for Savage at Hendon. The success of skywriting led Hinkler to the view that it might provide him with a living in Australia, and between 1924 and 1926 he tried to acquire the Australian rights from Savage and set up a small company to operate in his own country. Savage offered him the Australian rights on favorable conditions, but Hinkler was unable to raise the necessary capital. Throughout the years 1922 to 1933, Lingham made himself the indispensable "alter ego" of his employer, Savage, a role that Lingham saw without embarrassment as embracing both the business and domestic scenes. Lingham had no interest beyond his connection with the Savage family. In 1928 Jack Savage sent him to Australia, Lingham's interest in Jack's wife, Pauline, having become a little too close. Lingham operated his Skywriting SE5 from Coode Island in Melbourne at the time Hinkler was there. A unique friendship developed between Jack Savage and Bert Hinkler, and as a result, when Hinkler returned to England from the U.S.A. in 1932, he flew his Puss Moth from Southampton (where it had been left hangared) to Hendon Aerodrome and began his preparations for his big flight to Australia in the Sky-writing hangar. Business conditions were extremely bad and the Savage Skywriting Company seemed on the verge of collapse. Savage was in the U.S.A. looking for business when Hinkler arrived at Hendon, where Lingham was in charge of what he described as "a care and maintenance party." An ill-informed action by the Air Ministry had inflicted disaster on Savage from mid-1931 onwards, but a Parliamentary enquiry had come out strongly in his favour. Savage was struggling to get his business back on a proper footing, but it appeared, in September 1932, there was little prospect of success.

Hinkler worked on his aircraft at Hendon, and it was inspected there by Aeronautical Inspection Directorate officials and received its certificate of airworthiness in November 1932. A few days afterward the press announced that Bert Hinkler had been awarded the prestigious Johnston Memorial Trophy for navigation skill displayed during his 1931 flight across the South Atlantic and at other times. He was the only one at Hendon winning anything; day by day the position of Skywriting worsened.

So much for the names on the first list. What of the second list—those whom the press contacted for information when it was known Hinkler was overdue? Because the APA published the apparently prize piece of information that Hinkler had left his business affairs in the hands of a firm of solicitors, it might be thought that all APA reports to the Australian newspapers were the result of investigative reporting. On the contrary, the "firm of solicitors" report is quite singular. None of the remaining APA reports was in any way the result of investigative reporting; they were simply reports culled from the British newspapers day by day or based on material already held on file. This was quite a contrast with the Australian Cable Service, which interviewed Jack Savage as soon as it was known Hinkler was overdue. By Monday afternoon the ACS had also interviewed Dopey Lingham. This interview made front page headlines in the Sydney *Sun* on Tuesday, 10 January.

The two names that appear on both lists are Jack Savage and Dopey Lingham. They both match the characteristics of the APA informant, but they are nowhere mentioned by name in APA messages. The messages that identify them and associate their names with authentic information were sent to Australia by the ACS. If the informant was either Savage or Lingham, there has to be found some reason why their remarks on the "firm of solicitors" were sent to Australia via the alternative agency.

At this point the scene on Pratomagno, with the crashed aircraft and its missing propeller blade, comes back into our calculations. The loss in flight of a blade from this specific type of propeller assembly was singular in the experience of the manufacturer. If the singular condition had a singular cause, i.e., tampering, enquiries to establish the person responsible would have to begin at the hangar at Hendon where Hinkler kept his plane until a few hours before the flight, for there the aircraft was readily accessible. Though tampering cannot be proved on the basis of the propeller, because it is unavailable, the possibility of tampering points towards Hendon and the misuse of a particular skill.

There is a quite separate angle that points towards the Hendon hangar. It begins from a different direction. The mutual conduct of Katherine Hinkler and L. V. Pearkes postulates the existence of a plan based on prior awareness that Hinkler would meet his death on the flight. Their arrangement came into existence while the Puss Moth was still at Hendon. (It left Hendon in the forenoon of 6 January.) Neither of them had the technical knowledge or the level of access that would enable them to bring Hinkler's plane crashing. Some other, a third person, had to be involved, someone whose capability was of such a nature they could be assured Hinkler could be brought down. This adds two characteristics to those already adduced for the person who planted the false information with the press—Hendon and technical skill.

If the misleading information that Hinkler appointed a firm of solicitors on the eve of his departure can be traced back to the Hendon hangar, the place to which all suspicions must point as to its origin in any case, would it not suggest the answer to these other questions as well? Was there a person at the Hendon hangar who possessed the skill and knowledge of an airman and in whom a press reporter could also have absolute confidence as a person knowledgeable and authoritative as to what Hinkler might have done on the eve of his departure and who was also in a position himself to be the recipient of confidential information from Hinkler?

This brings Dopey Lingham and Jack Savage into dual focus. Witnesses to Hinkler's departure, who could be accepted by any pressman as his closest associates, they also controlled the hangar where the plane was prepared. Lingham actually comes into a triple focus for he was at the aerodrome in Australia where an attempt had been made on Hinkler's life in 1928.

It was the first time since Coode Island in 1928 that Hinkler, his aircraft, Dopey Lingham, and a Skywriting SE5 had been at the same aerodrome together. And a somewhat similar situation existed: Hinkler receiving publicity for his every move without seeking it, while Skywriting, which needed good publicity, was languishing for want of it.

There is one clue that identifies the "third person" who planted the information on the press about the firm of solicitors. In earlier reporting, while Hinkler was still preparing his plane, there had been at least two instances where a British newspaper, or newspaper columnist, alluded to an Australian, or a friend, as the source of reports that they made use of. There was to be a further instance. In the issue of the *Manchester Guardian* for 13 January, a columnist commented on the passing scene and in respect to Bert Hinkler said:

# HOW HINKLER DEPARTED

An Australian friend tells me that Hinkler's reticence, increased by disappointment over his continued failure to obtain regular aerial employment, has deepened latterly into an almost morbid habit of secrecy. His projected route to Australia, about which he made such a mystery, divulging it to nobody except his solicitors, proves now to have been only the ordinary track followed by aviators. Even his closest associates were kept in ignorance of his plans. Major Savage and Captain Lingham, the skywriters, who saw him off at Feltham in the darkness of Saturday morning, did not know until three or four hours before that he was leaving, and when he was asked at the aerodrome about passing the Customs he replied, "That's all right, they'll be here." Major Savage and Captain Lingham arranged motor car headlights so as to illuminate the fairway, and a moment or two later heard the engine of the Puss Moth roaring down the track. At the end of the lighted path they caught through the mist a faint glimpse of the aeroplane rising into the moonlight above. That was the last seen of Hinkler.

One friend who is missing Hinkler is a crippled black cat which he regarded as his mascot. He rescued it from a rabbit-trap in a wood near his home at Southampton, and tended its broken leg until it could get about again. The cat became firm friends with the marmoset which Hinkler brought with him in the plane on the great flight from South America, and they used to play about the house together until the marmoset succumbed last year in the rigours of the English climate. Mrs. Hinkler is in New Zealand, and the neighbours daily visit the house to feed the cat, which refuses to desert its home.

The human interest story on the cat, Mickey, can be disregarded. (It was reported in Australia by newspapers receiving ACS messages.) The "Australian friend" is a singular person who links a whole series of significant ideas. Note the range—the appointment of solicitors, Hinkler's morbid secrecy, absence of Customs, secrecy over route, the route known only to solicitors, closest associates Major Savage and Captain Lingham left in ignorance.

The inner meaning of the *Manchester Guardian* article starts to unravel at the point where it asserts that Hinkler's route was known only to solicitors. Only one person promoted that peculiar view: the reporter who sent the information through the Australian Press Association that Hinkler appointed solicitors on the eve of his departure. This reporter is therefore the Australian friend referred to by the *Manchester Guardian* columnist.

He is also the source of the report published in some Australian newspapers—those that received Australian Cable Service items—in which Hinkler's departure was described by Lingham. The point about Customs was set out in full in the Sydney *Sun* of 10 January. Lingham said, "I had previously asked Hinkler about the Customs. He replied, 'That is all right. They will be here.' As Hinkler prepared to depart, and the Customs men were absent we learned, in conformity with his usual taciturnity, that he had passed the Customs at Croydon on Friday."

Jack Savage's name is introduced into the *Manchester Guardian* account, but all the comments on Hinkler's departure derive from Lingham. Savage knew Hinkler was heading for Athens via Brindisi and had given him messages for relatives in Australia. The allegations all trace back to Lingham; Savage had nothing to do with them. The reporter who interviewed Lingham apparently did not know what Jack Savage had said twenty-four hours earlier.

To this point five facts have been established with certainty. The Australian reporter is the one who supplied the report to the Australian press about the solicitors. He used the APA. He sent a different account through the ACS. This was Lingham's description of Hinkler's takeoff, and it made a front-page headline in the Sydney *Sun* on 10 January. Lingham was his sole informant on Hinkler's departure, and Savage had nothing to do with it.

This clears the way to establishing where the "firm of solicitors" report originated.

There is residual information in the *Manchester Guardian* article that did not appear in the Australian press. This is the portion that asserted that Hinkler's reticence had developed into a morbid habit of secrecy and that Hinkler had not told Lingham his route. There are five significant elements:

• Lingham said Hinkler was morbidly secretive.
• Lingham said he had not been told the route.
• The solicitors only were told the route.
• The information on the solicitors was sent to Australia via the APA.
• Other information from Lingham was sent to Australia via the ACS.

These link into, and explain, each other with the addition of but two words:

• *Lingham said* the solicitors only were told the route.

The picture is clear. If what Lingham said was true, he could only have received the information on the solicitors as a confidence from Hinkler. As Hinkler was, according to Lingham, morbidly secretive and might yet reappear, he would regard Lingham's action as a breach of trust. It was perfectly natural, in these circumstances, for the reporter to suppress Lingham's name as the source and separate his information on the solicitors from his information on Hinkler's takeoff by sending one report via the ACS and one via the APA. This effectively concealed the connection.

There was one single Australian reporter. He had one sole informant. The deviousness with which the information was imparted by Lingham required little more than the giving of a name and a telephone number to the reporter with a statement accompanying it: "Don't ever say you got it from me."

The possibilities concerning Hinkler's fate that were coursing through Lingham's mind some fifty hours after the takeoff would have been endless. He had to remain anonymous or face possible exposure. Jack Savage would know Hinkler had left no such message during the period at Fairey's aerodrome, and there was also the possibility Hinkler might have escaped death and would expose the situation if he returned.

Corroboration of the "accuracy" of Lingham's information was easily achieved. All the reporter had to do was to telephone the firm of solicitors: there was no onus on Pearkes to assert a claim, produce credentials, or withstand challenges. Pearkes simply had to affirm that the information was correct. This was "corroboration." The reporter himself subsequently gave the story another twist when, after Shell Mex released details of Hinkler's route, he represented in his report to Australia that the APA had been specially favoured by the solicitor because the information sent to Australia on the route had come from the solicitor. Demonstrably it came from Shell Mex, but that would not have been evident in Australia to those reading newspapers subscribing to the APA service. Apparently the reporter felt it necessary to give the solicitor some kind of positive role.

Why did the reporter go along with what could be considered deviousness? The answer is in the phrase "morbidly secretive." If Hinkler was genuinely morbidly secretive, he would be most unhappy to find, if and when he reappeared, that his private information had been given out and published during his absence for all the world to read.

Only a person known to have been in contact with Hinkler over an extended period of time would be able to assert, truthfully or falsely, that Hinkler's reticence had "deepened latterly" into an almost morbid habit of secrecy, and have it accepted. Jack

Hinkler at Hendon late in 1932. On the left is C. G. Allen, well-known in England at the time for his pioneering experiments with television and wireless reception and transmission. Allen is demonstrating a portable wireless set.

Savage spoke in quite different terms of Hinkler, and Savage's wife, Pauline, was also much concerned for Bert Hinkler and the dangers he would face on the route. The person who made the statement to the Australian reporter was Dopey Lingham.

Lingham was the third man in the trio that acted from the outset on the basis of a prior and organised awareness that Hinkler's life was in danger on the flight. There is only one way Lingham could have developed such an awareness: he was the man who understood the possibilities. He was the man who tampered with Bert Hinkler's machine. Hinkler had nothing to do with the appointment of Pearkes who, from his known conduct, was some sort of angle in a triangle. Pearkes, in his turn, showed himself a lapdog for Katherine in all his activity and used his legal status to ensure that Hinkler was disposed of without too many questions being asked.

# Hendon Aerodrome

Hendon aerodrome with an air pageant in progress in the early 1930's. The Skywriting accommodation is clearly evident. The coloured smoke used by aircraft of the Royal Air Force for Hendon aerobatic displays was supplied by Skywriting. *Flight*

Hendon was established as a private aerodrome in the earliest days of flying in Britain. The Air Ministry took control of the aerodrome during World War I and the R.A.F. retained control thereafter for the duration of Hendon's existence as a flying field.

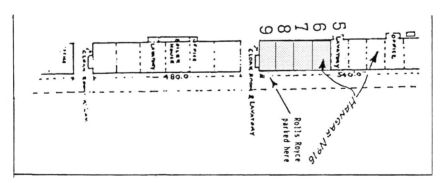

Portion of the Hendon Aerodrome ground plan. Skywriting, as pictured above, occupied bays 5–9 of Hangar 16. As far as can be ascertained, Hinkler occupied bay 6, marked with the letter T. (The Rolls Royce referred to on the plan is pictured overleaf.)

View from in front of the Skywriting office from bay 9 towards bay 5. The Rolls Royce is the one used by Jack Savage to light the runway at Fairey's aerodrome for Hinkler's takeoff.

# G. A. Lingham at Coode Island, 1928

G. A. Lingham and his Skywriting
SE5A at Larkin's Coode Island
aerodrome, Melbourne, in 1928.

# 14

# A LAST WORD

The essential facts of Hinkler's last flight can now be fully outlined. His intention was to complete a round-the-world flight, the first by light aeroplane, by flying from England to Australia, then continuing to Canada. He would thus arrive back at the point from which his flight across the South Atlantic began in 1931. Completion of this solo epic would crown him with the laurel wreath as a pioneering aviator and place him in a class of his own among world airmen. Prospects of such success would not be welcomed by all. Hinkler could well expect animosity and jealousy from some, particularly airmen unable to achieve similarly for themselves.

Hinkler had two "secrets." One related to his domestic situation, the other related to what he intended to do after he reached Australia. He thought more than he spoke, and he was of an uncommunicative, but not unfriendly, disposition. His mother's reaction to the news of his 1932 association with Katherine and of his intention to continue that association, had been a blow he felt keenly.

Hinkler's flight ended suddenly in Italy because of a propeller blade retention failure—a circumstance unique in the experience of the manufacturer of that specific type of blade. Given Hinkler's experience and the care with which he prepared his aircraft, the cause of such a malfunction demands the most intense scrutiny. He had hardly left England, for all purposes, when the incident occurred.

After Hinkler was missing for more than 48 hours, it was asserted by a person whose identity was not revealed by a news reporter that before he'd departed Hinkler had taken a step totally incompatible with his established solo practices and actions by appointing a "firm of solicitors" to look after his "business" affairs. There was no business to manage. With every mile flown by Hinkler the solicitor would have been that much further from where any "business" might be conducted, and it would remain that way throughout. In the early period while Hinkler was missing it was uncertain if he might suddenly show up. In this period the solicitor remained out of the limelight. The description "firm of solicitors" shielded his name in even those few instances where the newspapers hinted at his existence. He promoted no search activity. The only authority he held in this period was the authority of the "widow"—at least seven days before she could reasonably be assured she was a widow. Hinkler eventually was found to have died intestate—a peculiar situation for an aviator departing on a dangerous flight who supposedly had a solicitor as his business agent.

The will, if Hinkler left one, was most likely to be in his house, now unoccupied, at Southampton. In an attempt to locate personal documents belonging to Hinkler, persons unknown, whose interests were identical with the interests of Katherine Hinkler and Pearkes, travelled a considerable distance by car and ransacked the house on Sunday evening, 15 January 1933. In the course of the ransacking, opportunity was taken by one intruder to grind a heel into a photograph of Bert Hinkler's mother, an action indicating personal animosity. Hell hath no fury . . .

The early hour at which the false claim was asserted that Hinkler had appointed the solicitor to act as his agent, taken together with the known subsequent conduct of the legal widow and the solicitor, betrays an expectancy on their part—preceding Hinkler's departure—that Hinkler would not survive the flight. They capitalised on prior knowledge. Only one reason can account for such prescience—they knew that Bert Hinkler's plane had been tampered with.

The solicitor did not know the colour of Bert Hinkler's aircraft. He had not seen Bert Hinkler since World War I. He was not appointed by Bert Hinkler. Without question, however, he and the widow had been in close touch before she became a widow, for he and the widow were joined with the glue of mutual concord in the pursuit of their aims.

Neither the solicitor nor the legal widow could have been responsible for the tampering. This points to the existence of a third person who possessed the opportunity and the skill. Neither the legal widow nor the solicitor could have provided the spurious information to the press about Hinkler appointing a firm of solicitors and have had it accepted without question or challenge. This must have also emerged from a third person who possessed certain characteristics.

The third person in both cases is G. A. Lingham. It can be no one else. Lingham participated in a subterfuge that was based on his awareness that Hinkler's life was in danger on the flight. He had a very specific reason for this foreknowledge. He was the one responsible. He is the one who tampered with the Puss Moth or, more specifically, with its propeller, while it was in the Hendon hangar.

The identification of Lingham as the third person is made possible by the Achilles' heel that developed in the arrangements. Had the solicitor been able to assume control of Hinkler's affairs in a normal way, as he'd intended, he would not have come to public notice until his position was secure and he could act on the authority of the legal widow, that is, after Hinkler was known to be dead. His false claim had to be asserted prematurely, publicly, and deviously, thus opening a chink in the arrangements that had already been put in place.

The assertion was accepted and circulated by a reporter in London who supplied information to Australian news services. His source was not specified but can be identified. Lingham, in feeding the false information to the reporter, had to remain anonymous for two reasons: Hinkler might still have reappeared, and Lingham's statement could have been challenged by Jack Savage, had he been aware who made it, because Savage and Lingham were together with Hinkler at the time of his departure.

An attempt had been made on Hinkler's life in 1928 in Australia. A person who was present at the same aerodrome at the same time, namely Dopey Lingham, was also present in the hangar at Hendon in which Hinkler prepared his aircraft for the final flight in 1933. Under other circumstances this might have been a coincidence, a most unique coincidence. Or it might not. The physical actions needed to create the sabotage of Hinkler's air-craft—the Avian in 1928 and the Puss Moth in 1933—were little more than actions that in everyday situations are perfectly normal and innocent, such as tamping a pipe or tightening a nut. In each instance there was a lack of certainty as to where the aircraft would come down because the sabotage did not attain its peak of effectiveness until time had passed with the aircraft airborne. A blocked oil line and a propeller blade or fitting put under stress would both bring an aircraft down, but only after a period of flying.

In 1928, after complaining to Savage in a letter that Hinkler's absence in another state was holding things up, Lingham so arranged his own affairs as to be absent from the aerodrome in Melbourne after Hinkler returned, at the time when the blocked oil line would bring Hinkler's aircraft down. Fortunately for Hinkler, the blockage was discovered by his brother Jack. The Hinkler family were conscious from that time onwards of the possibility of sabotage.

From the moment in 1933 when Hinkler took off for Australia, a tight ring of three—"Hinkler's close associate," "Hinkler's solicitor," and "Hinkler's widow"—acted in concert on the basis of a prior and organised awareness that Hinkler would not be returning safely from the flight.

Hinkler's Puss Moth was in the Skywriting hangar from mid-September 1932 until 6 January 1933, a little more than one hundred days. His aircraft when it arrived at Hendon still bore the name apparent on its cowling after the 1931 flight—*Karohi*. In this era several leading aviators named their aircraft for friends or wives: Broadbent named his *DABS* after his deceased friend D. A. B. Smith, the Chinese characters on C. W. A. Scott's Gipsy Moth spelt his wife's name *Kathleen*, Melrose called his aircraft after his mother, *My Hildebrande*. Although Hinkler said the name *Karohi* was Maori for "lone hand," almost certainly he had named the aircraft for Katherine, the "HI" representing his own name and the first four letters Katherine and her maiden name.

(This assessment of the meaning of *Karohi* was divulged by the author in 1983 to a film producer who had no knowledge on the topic. The information was subsequently used in private conversation by the film producer and attributed by others to him.)

Hinkler removed the name *Karohi* from the cowling of the Puss Moth some time before it left the Hendon Skywriting hangar on 6 January 1933, in the lead-up to the final takeoff. This is evident from the cowling of the wrecked aircraft. The removal spells out something significant: the state of Bert Hinkler's mind.* He had often been asked what *Karohi* stood for. Apparently he had no liking to answer questions of that nature in Australia on his arrival at the end of the flight.

During the time Hinkler was at the Hendon hangar, anyone wishing to contact him would have had to ring Colindale 6075, the Skywriting number, or call at the hangar. For the first two months—until the middle of November 1932—Jack Savage was in the U.S.A. and Lingham was the "care and maintenance party" at Skywriting's Hendon office. If Katherine Hinkler called there or telephoned Bert Hinkler, Lingham would have been aware immediately and it would not have taken him long to work out the connection, even were it not revealed by the caller. Nothing is established on this aspect, but the possibilities are obvious. What is established is that, though he and Katherine had different reasons, on one aim there was a true marriage of their two minds. It would have taken no more than a few words, a chance phrase perhaps about persons having their names removed, to have led to a discussion of more serious import on the same theme and the realisation that their two minds did think alike. Contrary to impressions that may be held, no more than five or six sentences would have been needed to seal the compact. It simply required the name of a third person to whom enquiries could be referred after Hinkler left England. As the event developed, that name had to be given to a reporter rather prematurely.

A somewhat bizarre situation arose after Hinkler's crashed aircraft was found in Italy. It was generally thought that Hinkler crashed head-on into the mountain in bad weather. When an official finding was given, it attributed the crash to a different and equally wrong reason. It was therefore subsequently possible for

*Note the connections which tell the hidden story: Removal of the name 'Karohi' from the aircraft; the obliterated surname in the passport; and the photograph in the ransacked house with the face trodden in. All are directly connected with the marriage.

the perpetrator of the tampering to live out his life with an easy conscience, unaware that his tampering was the effective cause of Hinkler's crash and death. Not so for Katherine Hinkler and L. V. Pearkes, neither of whom needed to know anything more at the time than that Hinkler would not be returning safely from the flight, and that this eventuated.

Since his death on Pratomagno, Bert Hinkler has continued to reappear. At his funeral two generals were numbered with his pallbearers, a unique honour for an untutored Australian of a working-class family born in a country town. A fine marble memorial was erected as a spontaneous tribute on the mountain top overlooking the place where his body was found. In the course of time a second memorial was created to replace the first. In 1969 the aviation magazine *Flight International*, in the issue celebrating its own Diamond Jubilee, named Bert Hinkler as one of the twelve immortals of all-time aviation. The home at Southampton in which Hinkler lived, and which he named after the Bundaberg beach where he had experimented with his early gliders, was demolished in Southampton, taken to Bundaberg in Queensland, and there reerected in 1984. It has become a splendid attraction for visitors to the sugar city and—as far as is known—is only the second house to be reerected in Australia after transfer from England for reasons of history. This was the house that was ransacked in a search for documents in 1933. Bert Hinkler's name and achievements also featured in Australian Bicentenary celebrations in 1988, with a major air race in his honour.

Had Bert Hinkler succeeded in his attempt to land on the side of the mountain, he would have had very little chance of proving anything against anyone, whatever he suspected. The extended period of uncertainty as to his fate provided a stage on which the central actors could emerge and play out the themes and guidelines that governed their conduct. It is the pattern to be discerned in their conduct that provides the revelation. Disaster was in store for Hinkler, one way or another, and it was only a matter of time before it befell him.

The combination of circumstances that helped confuse the issues surrounding Bert Hinkler's last flight is unique from many standpoints. There was a long sequence of unusual and unexpected events—the way most newspapers immediately and incorrectly named Feltham as Hinkler's starting point instead of Fairey's aerodrome, which was in the same general area; Air Ministry incompetence and the failure by the press to penetrate that incompetence to elicit exactly what Hinkler had told the Ministry; the consequent criticism of Hinkler instead of the Air Ministry by the press; the long silence while Hinkler was missing and the sudden finding of the wreckage that served to bring the central characters onto the stage; the isolated region where the crash occurred; the unique topography of the crash site that spoke louder than words as to the reasons for the crash; the unexpectedly spontaneous and magnificent Italian tributes and the way these tributes set the pace for Australian politicians (who are hardly noted for such attitudes); the high profile that the reburial issue then created for Nancy, who was clearly unaware of Bert Hinkler's 1932 change of status; and finally, the erroneous official statements on the technical causes of the crash. The traditional view of Hinkler's last flight, which derives from the misinformation attendant upon these circumstances, is completely upside down. It requires the uncritical acceptance of features that are fundamentally foreign to Hinkler's established modes of conduct as a responsible pioneering airman.

The high regard in which Hinkler was held as an airman is reflected in the glowing tributes paid to him by the aviation correspondents of the press. At Southampton, where he was well known, the *Southern Daily Echo* commented:

> Hinkler was an air pilot of surprising versatility. His piloting skill was allied to veritable genius as a mechanic and an almost uncanny ability as a navigator. Hinkler, it has been said, was clearly not an ordinary mortal. He appeared to have a genius—amounting almost to a sixth sense—for discovering navigational facts about which the average pilot would only be able to satisfy himself by means of elaborate tests.
>
> Add to the abovementioned qualities indomitable courage, undefeatable optimism, and resourcefulness in an emergency, and one arrives at some understanding of the secret of this remarkable man's success in the sphere of aviation.

In part the article reflected comments that had been published earlier by the London *Times*.

Earlier, the magazine *Flight* had written of him: "As a pilot it is hardly possible to rate Hinkler too high. Personal friends may be accused of bias if they give him first place among the pilots of the British Empire, but in sober fact his claim to that position can hardly be disputed. . . . "

The same writer, Hinkler's long-time acquaintance Maj. F. A. de V. Robertson, paid him a lengthy tribute in the *Manchester Guardian*, which began:

Bert Hinkler, who, it is now established, met his death in a crash in the Apennines, I think it is fair to say, was the greatest all-round pilot of the British Empire in the dozen years which followed the Armistice.

Among other things, Major Robertson said:

With all these grounds for pride, he was the most modest and unassuming of men. He shunned publicity; perhaps he shunned it overmuch. Sometimes he tried to make money, but his motive never was greed or love of gold for its own sake. He wanted money solely to give practical expression to his own ideas of what a touring aeroplane ought to be. His personal tastes were of the simplest, and his shabby clothes were a characteristic feature of his charming personality. He was a delightful companion, with a gift of whimsical humour which showed the quickness of his mind in all emergencies. To these qualities must be added a great practical knowledge of engines and high technical skill. . . . I do not think anyone ever got him to talk about his war experiences. He suddenly became famous with his flight to Turin, and between his great flights he always lapsed into obscurity. He was one of the toughest and most enduring men Australia ever turned out. In appearance he was short, and I might describe him as fascinatingly ugly, but his smile would have dispelled the deepest gloom. I wonder if we shall ever again see in one man so many of the qualities which go to make a really great pilot.

Since his takeoff into destiny on 7 January 1933, Bert Hinkler's final flight has been surrounded by mystery and misrepresenation. The man in the best position to provide the answers and dispel the mystery, George Alexander Lingham, will not be remembered for himself. That he was not called upon to provide the answers is a matter for regret. The opportunity arose, but those authorities who were provided with the opportunity made no use of it. Beyond that, it is possible for no man to go.

*    *    *

In June 1933, Lingham's employment with Skywriting came to an end. After World War II, he continued with the aviation company Hestair and with Savage & Parsons as a director. Jack Savage died in 1945. On Tuesday, 19 December 1950, at noon at Caxton Hall, Lingham married Pauline Savage.

In Pauline's diary the name used for Lingham, her new husband, is not Dopey, but Alex. In part they had access to separate residences. Lingham's diary refers to Pauline simply as "MD." Pauline continued to refer to Jack Savage in her diary as "My Darling." It does not need a genius to work out what the initials MD in Lingham's diary stand for. On 23 April 1958, while suffering from the illness that proved terminal, Pauline wrote in her diary: "This is the anniversary." "The" was underlined several times. It was on 23 April that Jack Savage and Pauline were married. On 21 October 1958, Pauline wrote: "My darling's birthday. Sheila rang. She doesn't forget her daddy."

Pauline Savage died in hospital on Friday, 15 July 1960. Lingham, almost forty years after his first meeting with Jack Savage, became the possessor of the Savage fortunes.

After Lingham's death in July 1982, at the age of eighty-three—he was born in Melbourne, Australia, in 1898—a strange discovery was made. Lingham left the accumulated fortune to his own distant relatives, who accepted the financial endowment—which was considerable—but not personal items. The few Savage items left unsold by Lingham became the property of the Savage family.

The items proved intriguing. In the early years of his marriage Jack Savage had presented Pauline with a silver cigarette case that bore his initials. Soon afterwards Lingham also made a present to Pauline of a silver cigarette case. It bore his initials.

Presumably, after Pauline's death in 1960, in the tenth year of the marriage entered into with Lingham, he would have become aware of the entries in her diary in which she quite naturally alluded to Jack Savage as "My Darling." Lingham's imitative "MD"

140

had not erased Jack Savage from her memory or affections. In his ambition to be Jack Savage's alter ego, Dopey Lingham had failed this final test.

The silver cigarette cases that came to Savage's children on the death of Lingham seemed to say much of what Lingham had been thinking. An attempt—a considerable attempt—had been made to erase the "J.C.S." from the cigarette case that Jack presented to his wife. The "G.A.L." case was unmarked.

How much does this tell us about Lingham? It was to Jack Savage that he owed everything. Without Jack Savage, Lingham was nothing. Yet he had tried to erase the name of such a man from memory. The scraping and scratching action that was necessary to do so had a malign intent but would, in most other cases, have been a quite natural and innocent action.

Just like tamping a pipe.

Or overtightening a nut.

*   *   *

Katherine Hinkler died in the United States in 1976. (She was not a U.S. citizen. Her given name was recorded as Catherine, and her signature featured an apparent initial C, which was made into K by the addition of a stroke.) Leslie V. Pearkes, solicitor, died in England a decade later aged ninety. For much of their lives after 1933 they stayed in touch.

The unknown Australian reporter remains unidentified. His attributes indicate that he was energetic, career-bent, and gullible. Such attributes point to a young man, probably in his early twenties. Perhaps he may not have continued a career in journalism but turned to other pursuits. Fifty or more years later he could still be alive. In his notebook or diary, if they survive, or in his memory if he survives, there will be the name of a person whom he interviewed on Monday morning, 9 January 1933, who told him that Hinkler had appointed a "firm of solicitors . . . on the eve of his departure." The name of that informant, when it is retrieved from the past, will confirm how it came about that three people were able to act in concord with prescience of the disaster that would overtake Bert Hinkler, and why it was that Bert Hinkler's aircraft was found with a metal propeller blade missing from its hub.

When that name reemerges, Bert Hinkler's final flight will at last be over.

## Authority to Investigate

79 Lapraik St
Albion
Brisbane
25-11-68.

To whom it may concern:

I am the brother of the long distance aviator Bert Hinkler (1892- 1933)

Mr L a. Cordingley has my permission to investigate the circumstances relating to the missing propeller blade of my brother's crashed Puss-moth. aircraft.

J. Hinkler.

Laurie Cordingley, a friend of the author, was on a visit to England at the time enquiries concerning the propeller became necessary. He agreed to assist. The author sought and received from Bert Hinkler's brother, Jack, a written authority for the enquiries. At a later stage three attempts to have the circumstances of Bert Hinkler's last flight investigated officially met with negative responses.

# Appendices

# *Appendix 1*

# THE FLYING KANGAROO

The kangaroo is now a distinctive feature on many Australian aeroplanes. Since Qantas first asserted a role as the national flag carrier at the end of World War II its aircraft have been readily identifiable at international airports by the kangaroo prominently visible on the tail fin.* For a number of years the Qantas kangaroo was provided with wings, but the more recent version lacks such equippage. When the internal carrier, Trans Australia Airlines, switched its name to Australian Airlines in 1986, it also reverted to an earlier use of the kangaroo as an adornment on its aircraft. The defence forces—navy, army, and air force—have found the kangaroo a usefully distinctive symbol of nationality.

Discussion has arisen at times as to which Australian flying organisation can claim precedence in the use of this feature.

It seems that pride of place should belong to the Australian Army. In the 1914–18 war the Australian Flying Corps, which was part of the Australian Imperial Force, had four squadrons in the field—number 1 in Palestine and numbers 2, 3, and 4 over the Western Front. Number 6 Squadron, Australian Flying Corps, was a training squadron based at Minchinhampton in England. Photographs of 6 Squadron aircraft in 1918 show each to be decorated with a kangaroo on the side of the fuselage. While individual members of the flying corps in earlier days may possibly have added a small kangaroo to the markings of their own aircraft, the widespread use by 6 Squadron seems to be the first on an officially accepted basis. There had been some use in France by Australian airmen of the boomerang as a motif, the appeal in that instance being that a boomerang is usually made to return.

*The kangaroo was first used on a Qantas aircraft in October 1944.

# The Flying Kangaroo

Bert Hinkler with an early Avro aircraft bearing a winged kangaroo and the letters "M A" inside a circle. The origin of what seems to be a company motif is unknown, but—to judge from Hinkler's attire—some importance attached to the occasion.

The rudder of the Avro Baby in 1921. On the 1920 flight to Turin the rudder also featured a kangaroo inside the "G."

The SE5 of Lt. R. M. Douglas bearing the standard kangaroo as depicted on aircraft of No. 6 Squadron, A.F.C., in 1918.

In 1919 the Australian government announced a prize for the first Australian to fly home from England within a total of thirty days. Two of the machines entered in this "race" bore appropriate names—the Sopwith Wallaby and the Blackburn Kangaroo. These names, however, did not continue as established aircraft types, though the Kangaroo was initially produced as a bomber, of which twenty were built. Both aircraft crashed on the way to Australia—the Kangaroo in Crete and the Wallaby in the Dutch East Indies (Indonesia). The Sopwith Wallaby was subsequently shipped to Australia and there rebuilt. It went into commercial service for a time.

The honour of making an international civil flight in an aircraft adorned with a kangaroo seems almost certainly to belong to Bert Hinkler. When he flew from London to Turin in May 1920, his small biplane Avro Baby bore a kangaroo on each side of the rudder. It was painted inside the compulsory "G" marking. Hinkler's flight terminated at Rome and on his return to England he exhibited the Avro Baby at Olympia, where the kangaroo was plain for all to see. It was even plainer when Hinkler took part in an air race where the kangaroo was accompanied only by his racing number, 1. Hinkler brought the same aeroplane to Australia by ship in 1921 and the kangaroo again adorned the rudder, though this time the airman added a small drawing high on the fuselage near the cockpit of a black cat, doubtless for "good luck" purposes. He flew nonstop from Sydney to Bundaberg to visit his home.

On his return flight to Sydney in the Avro Baby in April 1921. Hinkler was accompanied by a caged magpie. After leaving Brisbane on 27 April, Hinkler encountered bad weather and landed on a beach in northern New South Wales to effect some repairs to his propeller. A beachgoer endeavoured to extract some information from him and the local newspaper account of the incident (which contains some minor descriptive and spelling errors) would have brought smiles to the faces of those familiar with Hinkler's attitudes. Note the concluding sentence:

> On Wednesday morning, at 10:30 A.M., an "Avro" airplane with the letters G.E.A.C.Q. on the body of the plane and A.G. on the tail, also the makers' name, A. V. Roe and Sons, and a kangaroo painted on the tail, landed on the beach at Broome's Head, south of the Clarence, directly in front of the week-enders' huts, which are now, of course, mostly deserted for the winter months. The airman was most reticent concerning himself, but stated that he had come from Brisbane, leaving there at 6 A.M. that day and was on his way to Sydney. He is probably the man who was forced to land at Newcastle on account of petrol shortage, since he seemed anxious to secure petrol. He landed at Broome's Head in order to repair the cloth covering of his propellor, which had become damaged in his long flight. The airman carried as a mascot a magpie in a wire cage strapped in the body of the machine. He stated that Broome's Head beach was a landing place par excellence. He was very enthusiastic on this point; in fact this was the only topic he would converse on.

Some time later the same morning Hinkler was forced to make a second beach landing at Anna Bay, north of Newcastle, when on the verge of complete loss of visibility in lashing rain. He landed safely but the machine was overturned soon after by strong winds. Hinkler trudged off, complete with caged magpie, looking for a friendly farmhouse. Fortunately he succeeded in his quest, and he and the damaged aircraft eventually arrived in Sydney. The Avro Baby remained in Australia when Hinkler returned to England, via Canada, but the kangaroo disappeared from its rudder and was lost to memory. The aircraft is now displayed in the Queensland Museum.

The place on the rudder where once there was in Hinkler's time the large registration letter "G" and the drawing of a kangaroo is now occupied by the monogram of J. J. Smith, a pioneer flyer and the final owner of the aeroplane. The presence of this monogram acknowledges in a practical manner Jim Smith's gesture in donating his aircraft to the museum, while retaining on his behalf his connection with Bert Hinkler. It both symbolises and makes tangible the camaraderie of the air, a change that would surely have won the approval, and no doubt the applause, of the great aviator himself.

# Appendix 2

# STEVE BROGDEN AND HAMBLE DAYS

Steve Brogden was a fitter at Hamble in the exciting years from 1921 to 1926, the time when Bert Hinkler was at his most active there as chief test pilot for A. V. Roe & Co., manufacturers of Avro aircraft. Late in the 1960s, at a time when most men would have been happy to enjoy a restful retirement, Steve Brogden undertook the task of recording the recollections of the surviving staff of the Hamble experimental establishment of the Avro Company. Undeterred by the cold and wet of English winter evenings, he made his way along Southampton lanes, knocking at the doors of otherwise obscure addresses. His companion on these ventures was Graham Jost, an Australian from Southampton University. The investigators received much moral support from Prof. Brian Clarkson of the Institute of Sound and Vibration Research at the University, and his secretary, Mrs. Jackie Halliday.* Steve Brogden had found useful employment at the university and was held in high regard.

Bert Hinkler arrived at Hamble in 1919. Though his postwar rehabilitation course required him to work "on the bench," he had a special arrangement with the management enabling him to fly the company's aircraft. At that time a fellow Australian, H. A. Hamersley, was chief test pilot. Terence B. Tully, an expert at sideslipping an aircraft onto the small Avro aerodrome and almost through the hangar doors, also carried out some testing. When Hamersley returned to the Royal Air Force and Tully left for Canada (ultimately to lose his life attempting an Atlantic flight), the way was open for Bert Hinkler to assume a flying role for the

---

*The chief technician at the institute, Mr. Henry Eales, and Mr. Charles Brocklesby of the geography department also were prominent in providing assistance.

company. He was chief test pilot from 1921 until the end of 1926, testing not only the experimental machines built at Hamble but also the production run from the Manchester factory. From the beginning of 1927—in circumstances that clearly left Bert Hinkler quite bitter—another pilot was appointed to the Manchester position. With little testing available at Hamble, Hinkler had to diversify and 1927 saw him flying autogyros developed by the Spaniard Juan La Cierva and also doing some testing of aircraft produced by other companies. Though bearing the name A. V. Roe, the company was really a totally owned subsidiary of Crossley Motors. Hinkler no longer had his own room inside the works but made casual use of a small external building occupied by the engineer in charge of flying operations. The year 1927 was a frustrating one in many other respects: Hinkler had hoped to fly to Australia but circumstances prevented it. Instead he pulled off a different coup by flying his Avro Avian biplane G-EBOV solo nonstop from England to Latvia and thereby set the aviation world on its ear. In an attempt to secure funds for an England-Australia flight, he attempted a record flight from England to India with a well-known pilot, R. H. McIntosh, in a single-engined Fokker late in 1927. Weather conditions forced them down in Poland, and they were lost to the outside world for several days. Contriving to escape imprisonment, they took to the air again and flew back to England. Hinkler made his successful solo flight to Australia in G-EBOV in February 1928 and was not seen again in England until late October of that year. Lord Wakefield welcomed Hinkler back with a major aviation celebration in London, for which the guest list totalled more than three hundred. Mindful of the interest of the Avro staff, past and present, in his flight in the Hamble-built Avro Avian to Australia, Bert Hinkler gave an illustrated lecture one evening in the staff canteen. That was a fitting finale; it marked the definitive end of his connection with the Avro Company. Armstrong Siddeley bought out Crossley Motors and A. V. Roe himself joined with a friend to form the Saunders-Roe Company, which had its base on the Isle of Wight. The Avro establishment began winding down and some of its draughting room staff were transferred to Manchester. In 1929–30 Hinkler and his friend Rowland Bound hired one of the small Avro buildings as a workshop for construction of the Ibis aircraft. The experimental establishment closed but there was a continued aviation existence when the owners of the company commenced operations as Air Service Training at the larger Hamble Aerodrome, which had come into operation. After he went to the U.S.A. in the latter half of 1930, Hinkler had very limited contact with his old Avro associates, Rowland Bound and a particular friend, Jim Laver, excepted. The Avro staff distributed themselves throughout the aviation industry in England, wherever they could find use for their skills.

It was Steve Brogden's task to locate as many former Avro staff in the Southampton region as he could. He was soon in touch with Jim Laver, a fitter who had left Hamble before Steve began there and who had more recently retired from his position in a shipping office. Those he contacted in the course of the enquiries included the following:

Jim Laver, fitter, 1919–21
Claude Bevis, fitter, 1915–26
Austin Burgess, rigger, 1912 throughout Hamble period.
Geoff Stride, senior draughtsman, 1924–28
Bill Henderson, wood worker, 1924–31
Jack Chouls, fitter, 1924–28
Bob Randall, fitter, 1918–27
Fred J. Harvey, fitter, 1921–23
John Dunkerton, coppersmith, 1915–25
Fred Bevis, transport manager (fifty years service in Hamble aviation)
J. W. (Henry) Dyer, draughtsman, 1921–29
Reg Hooker, apprentice, 1926–31
Jack Salter, various, 1919–31
Mabel Whitcombe (Murrant), canteen manageress, 1924–31
Bill Boxall, fitting shop foreman, 1920–30

They knew of Hinkler's various residences, the motorbikes and cars he drove, his spare time recreations, the pets of the Hinkler household, his work accommodation that changed so abruptly at the end of 1926. More generally they recalled incidents of the period, sometimes involving Hinkler, other times A. V. Roe himself, sometimes the staff on the works floor.

Within the large square building at Hamble were a drawing

office, fitting shop, machine shop, electrical shop, engine maintenance benches, and erecting areas for aircraft, with all the support functions such as propeller making provided for. There laboured each day fabric workers and riggers and skilled tradesmen of every description. The workshop carried no passengers. All were highly skilled men in the old tradition. The floor of the building was one of the best in the south of England, a type of parquetry. All the staff remembered that floor, just as they all marvelled more—as time passed—that aircraft had once taken off and landed on the small grassed strip between the back of the building and Southampton Water. On one occasion a flight of Avro 504s were forced to land on that small aerodrome, coming in with the wind behind them. As they touched down, over they went on their noses—1, 2, 3. . . .

The day in September 1922 that Avro Baby G-EAXL took off from the small Avro Aerodrome to finish its flight almost immediately in Southampton Water was a disappointment not only for Hinkler but also for Fred Bevis, who had endured a sequence of incidents in the previous twenty-four hours before the engine was installed in the aircraft. Bevis had driven from Hamble to Twickenham to pick up the engine. His vehicle broke its axle and he "cadged a lift" to Basingstoke, where he obtained an axle. Bevis worked throughout the night to repair his vehicle and reached Hamble in time for the Green engine to be installed into the aircraft at 6:00 A.M. Hinkler took off from the small aerodrome, the engine cut out soon after takeoff, and the Avro Baby went straight into the sea. Such were life's hopes and disappointments at an experimental establishment in the pioneering days. G-EAXL never flew again.

There were memorable, if not to say colourful, characters in those early days. They remembered Farmer Bartlett, whose cows grazed behind the factory when the small drome was not in use. The famous designer, Roy Chadwick, who lost his life when an Avro Tudor crashed in 1947, was recalled as a man who almost always wore spats; at least, that was the impression he created among some of the work staff. Chadwick certainly always bore a neat appearance. Jack Hudson, a woodworker of the highest repute, was a dour Yorkshireman who chewed tobacco and possessed innumerable pipes that he left lying about handy to any job he was working on, thereby ensuring a ready pipeful at all times. In 1929 Hudson worked for Hinkler on the Ibis at the airman's home at Thornhill.

Jack Bradbury, another craftsman in wood, was the propeller maker. Previously prepared wood sections were placed on top of each other, then he glued and pressed them. With gauges and measures he gave the propeller its shape, a procedure designed to ensure it was perfectly balanced. Bradbury's work included the four-bladed, sixteen-foot propeller for the one-thousand-horse-power Avro Aldershot, which Hinkler first tested in December 1922.

Coppersmith John Dunkerton had good cause to remember a Japanese delegation that arrived to inspect aircraft under construction. His copper ashtray served the normal practical purpose. But when they saw it, the Japanese deluged him with requests for similar ashtrays to take away as souvenirs. The skilled coppersmith became temporary artifact manufacturer. Dunkerton, at a later time, also made a copper kettle for Nancy Hinkler.

Young apprentices took every opportunity to get into the air, usually as ballast whenever an aircraft underwent a load test. Engineer Sam Hughes logged every flight. His office was an external building situated near the corner of the main Avro workshop, and his duties included "rounding up the young fellows who wanted to fly," as soon as the possibility of a load test arose. Almost all the staff flew with Hinkler at one time or another, including Mabel Whitcombe, the canteen manageress.

There was one very memorable crash on the small aerodrome. A director of Avro had been keen for a certain pilot to fly a specially strengthened small aircraft with a 450-horsepower engine in a major race. The pilot, who was recovering from injuries, was warned that after he took off from Hamble he should not attempt to return but should continue to a larger aerodrome a little distance away at Gosport and land there. However, soon after his departure, the staff heard him returning. They watched as he made "a perfect landing too far up the drome" and continued on into a railway cutting, from whence came crashing and rending noises. An ambulanceman, quickly on the scene, sighted the pilot in the

155

wreckage and called concernedly, "Are you all right, old man?" The response was rather imperious. "Don't you old man me. I'm a major." Whether deservedly or not, the crash added to the major's already existing injuries. His reply was immortalised in Hamble repartee.

The railway lines running to the cutting also provided a hazard of a different kind. A series of hedgerows were flattened and a new, larger aerodrome came into use in the mid-1920s on the other side of the road across from the factory. The fast, all-wooden Avenger fighter was being taxied on its way to the new larger aerodrome when the skid caught on the railway lines and pulled the tail off. Hinkler was not at the controls on that occasion.

When flying operations were transferred to the larger aerodrome, the Avro Ava torpedo bomber was taken there for testing. The Ava bogged and the torpedo was removed for return to the workshop. The trolley carrying the torpedo escaped its handlers as it entered the workshop gate, careering down the incline to the wall of the factory. Its forward motion suddenly being stopped, the trolley acted as a launch pad and the torpedo went spearing forward, stopping only when it rammed hard against the factory wall. None of the handlers were certain beforehand whether or not the torpedo had an explosive head, so the first successful demonstration of the Avro Company's torpedo-delivering capacity might very well have been a flattened Avro factory.

The Bison, a fleet spotter, was tested by Hinkler, but the steep fall of the engine cowling disoriented him in his landing approach. He had no sighting point. It was rigged with a bracket and a broom handle in an effort to overcome the problem, but this proved of little assistance and was removed soon after. Hinkler's shortness of stature was also a disadvantage with some of the larger aircraft. A supply of cushions kept in Sam Hughes's office helped minimise problems arising from his short leg length.

Experiments at Hamble were not concerned solely with aircraft. The petrol tank of the Avro Aldershot was covered with rubber. The thinking was that, if the tank was punctured, the rubber would close and act as a seal. One aircraft that experienced a short life was dubbed "the Venetian blind" because it had a number of wings like a series of slats. The apparent purpose of the design was to increase stability, but it saw no subsequent development.

Steve Brogden

# Test pilot at Hamble
## ...Viewpoints 1

"What I liked about Bert Hinkler was he knew exactly how to explain what the trouble was...We could say: if we do this, do you think it will do that? And you could talk to him, there was nothing that I could call hi-falutin about him."
(Fred Harvey, Fitter)

"A little chap came around one day and wanted to borrow a spanner, and I thought: Who the deuce is this chap? I didn't know who he was, so I said 'You can borrow it, but bring it back please, will you', and he said 'All right'. He brought it back and another time he wanted to borrow a rule and dividers...I didn't know who he was, and I said: 'Who's that fellow that keeps coming around?' He was about as tall as me, very sunburned, and looked a very fit man. I said: 'Who's he?' and they said 'That's Bert Hinkler, he's one of the test pilots here'. After a while we became familiar and I told him he'd better grow a little bit if he wanted to use a man's tools..." (Steve Brogden, fitter at Avros 1921-1926, 5ft 2ins in height. Hinkler was 5ft 4ins.)

"I remember Bert testing a very early autogyro. It had four rotor blades, and cables to keep them at their 90° spacing. Coming in to land, roughly about 800feet, one cable severed and naturally all the Rotors or blades tried to catch up with one another, all out of balance. Thanks to our friend (Bert) once more he got the gyro down without much damage but was bruised badly about the face..."
(Ron Cooper)

"He was a natty little man. He used to amuse everyone by his antics sometimes. I remember an occasion he landed there with an aircraft and the cowling in those days was not very secure. It was only just push in and pop round, and it had come adrift. He quickly got out of the cockpit and up there and tightened it all up again. Didn't shout for anybody, did it all himself. All those things sort of intrigued everybody, I think. The young men we sort of idolised him". (Jack Chouls)

"I remember we installed a new five-cylinder Armstrong Siddeley engine called a Mongoose. I occupied the front seat and we took off towards the Southampton Water. On reaching 800 or 900 feet in a climb the engine lost power. Bert had two chances - fall in the sea or return to the aerodrome. He did a type of a left-hand turn combined with a side slip. Anyway we made it, full marks to our Bert. We had slight damage to the undercarriage and both a little shaken". (Ron Cooper)

"My first recollection of Bert Hinkler was when he arrived at our main gate of the Experimental Avro Factory at Hamble on his wife's cycle, complete with a bag slung around his shoulders which contained Bert's dinner. I don't think our new test pilot had a lot to spare. We all soon came to know him; he was small in stature, he would have made a good jockey. He had a most charming smile, showing several of his gold teeth". (Ron Cooper)

*Hamble Memories*

"Not at any time do I ever remember him going off the deep end about anything". (Bob Randall, fitter)

"Very modest man, very modest. He was a very warm sincere character, I think. He was quite a character actually. Great sense of humour, too, and he had pretty good physical endurance. Because sometimes I've known, when he was preparing for a flight - when he was preparing particularly for the flight he made to Rome non-stop - and he would never stop. He'd often start work in the morning and he'd work right through to tea time. Not stop for lunch, probably eat a sandwich on the job..." (Claude Bevis, fitter at the Avro works 1915-1926)

"I never heard him raise his voice to anyone. Never. If he wanted to say anything it was a conversation". (Fred Harvey, fitter 1921-1923)

"He was never a chap to want to show off or be made a fuss of. He was very unassuming in nature, I think". (John Dyer, draughtsman)

"He couldn't reach the rudder bar - they had to make wooden blocks on the bar and they had to pad the seat; he had to have three or four cushions at the back and three or four underneath before he could see out of the thing". (Claude Bevis, discussing Hinkler's problems on a large bomber)

"He was not a fussy eater...He would eat what you put before him". (Mabel Whitcombe, canteen manageress)

"He was a decent type of fellow that you could converse with - not a snobbish type...He was very popular on the works side". (Austin Burgess)

"The first time I met Bert Hinkler was in 1919 at the Avro works. He was a test pilot and a good one. He used to take everything in his stride, consequently we all admired him. He always struck me as a person you could put some trust in". (Austin Burgess, a carpenter rigger at Avro works throughout Hinkler's period)

"He had these motorcycles. The first one was a vintage Triumph, a single-cylinder Triumph. The next one was a twin-cylinder Matchless with a huge spring frame, and of course he put this smaller (sleeve-valve) engine in and the ports of the sleeve used to coke up about every forty miles so if you went from here to Bournemouth, which we used to go on our motorbikes, you generally had about two stops where you dropped the sleeve down, knocked the ports out, and shoved it up again because they used to gum up...Certainly it was a very light thing you see, because it had no valve gear, no tappet gear or anything like that. Just this sleeve on the Daimler sleeve-principle...Then he had a car designed by A.V. Roe himself at one time, a car which had a flat floor to the body and the seats were bucket seats..." (Jim Laver)

"Bert came to Southampton, just before he left on his ill-fated flight, to say cheerio to some friends...He came into the office to me and we went out and had a cup of coffee together and I went down to the Floating Bridge - he was going back to Hamble to fly back to London - and there I left him and he went off on the Floating Bridge and I went back to the office". (Jim Laver, Avro fitter 1919-1921, and long-time friend of Bert Hinkler)

*Hamble Memories*

And so the stories went on. Of the range of incidents some were humorous, some serious. There was the lunch break when Steve Brogden was cleaning his bicycle and a challenge arose as to who was the more competent, Brogden or Bert Hinkler, to ride the other's motor bike or racing cycle. Both men were about the same height.* Hinkler's motorbike had a cushion instead of a seat to permit his feet to reach the ground. Brogden's racing bicycle had wooden rims, fixed wheel, no brakes, racing tyres, and dropped handlebars. Hinkler had no experience of such a bike so the result was inevitable. His head bumped up and down on the handlebars, his posterior rose and fell in rhythm with the unstoppable motion of the pedals, the bicycle took complete control and eventually Bert and bicycle collapsed in a heap on an embankment, the only means of bringing the performance to an end.

At lunch times Hinkler occasionally provided amusement for the staff. Placing a borrowed handkerchief in the middle of the small aerodrome, he would then fly circuits of the area, bringing his aircraft down to touch—first with one wheel then the other— the handkerchief as it lay on the ground. "I always pretend I haven't got an engine," he confided to a fellow airman, impressed with his ability, to whom he introduced the game.

All acknowledged Hinkler's methodical approach to his task. Austin Burgess taught him wire splicing. Hinkler thought it a valuable skill to possess if he found himself alone and in difficulty. So it was in everything he undertook. The workshop tribute to his comprehensive preparations actually took the form of a joke. "But he's forgotten his sickle," said one wit, as Hinkler departed on his flight to Australia in 1928. "And what would he need a sickle for?" his surprised workmate responded. "Well, what will happen if he comes down in a field of corn?" the wit dryly retorted.

Bert Hinkler's ingenuity and interests were not restricted to aeroplanes and aero engines. He conceived various devices to try out on his motor car engines. One of Hinkler's petrol-saving attempts brought the suggestion from Fred Bevis that Hinkler had finally succeeded in running his car on hot air. Hinkler was always interested in photography and he had a super Zeiss lens in his own camera and a self-made enlarger.

*Hinkler was 5 ft. 4 ins.; Brogden was 5 ft. 2 ins.

Before going to live at Thornhill in 1926, Hinkler had lived at three other places within easy reach of Hamble. On first arriving after World War I, he found digs at Netley. His next residence was in Southampton at Havelock Road near the Civic Centre, in an area apparently known as the Polygon, with a nearby hotel of the same name. After that he went to Hedge End for several years. There was space for a tennis court and a large garden with fruit trees at Hedge End, and he kept a few ducks and some hens as well. The Hedge End house still stands; at that time it was in a remote area.

While at Hedge End he developed great interest in radio and even built some powerful receivers with a range as far as his homeland and these gave him recreation and pleasure. Visitors to Hedge End, who sometimes encountered lengths of wiring over the stairways, chicken houses, tennis court, and other parts of the house, may not have been as enthusiastic for his projects as Hinkler was, particularly if they had been looking forward to a game of tennis. One of Hinkler's radio friends, C. G. Allen, was also an early experimenter with television. In 1929, while flying over London in an aircraft piloted by Hinkler, Allen created a long-distance reception record by picking up a broadcast from Melbourne, Australia.

In the neighbouring house there lived a young boy, Fred Sharpe, who took a great interest in Hinkler's doings. (Years later he gave a first-hand description of Hinkler's procedure in dropping bags of wood chips to Nancy as he flew overhead. She laid out a marker on the ground for Hinkler to aim at. One type of Avro aircraft in use at that time could remain airborne at about 40 mph, so the exercise was not as dangerous as it might otherwise seem, though it was certainly not one to be indulged in by a pilot unsure of his own ability.) An impression that lingered in young Fred's mind was of Hinkler riding "a crock" motorcycle with big handlebars. Hinkler had two motorbikes that were remembered, a Triumph and a Matchless, and three small cars. The first car was an experimental type, originally owned—and apparently designed—by A. V. Roe himself. Then there was a Willys Overland with a "dicky" seat, and this was followed by a smart Riley. The Riley came into Hinkler's possession after he went to live at Thornhill.

The Thornhill house was built in a copse a short way off the Southampton-Portsmouth Road. He solved the problem of an entrance to the house through the copse by purchasing brick rubble. Jim Laver helped him turn the brick rubble into an acceptable roadway. Nancy Hinkler was remembered by those who came to know her, as dark-haired and a little taller than Bert. The neighbouring property was owned by a farmer named Stride, and the Hinkler household received its milk and eggs from this source. There was another home at a distance that was referred to as "the keeper's cottage" and there resided Mr. and Mrs. Hallett. There were gravel pits in the vicinity of the copse.

After the construction of the Ibis aircraft reached a certain stage, the use of the Avro workshop was dispensed with and the work continued at Hinkler's house. Hinkler towed the frame of the Ibis from Hamble to Thornhill behind his Riley car. Jack Hudson and John Dunkerton put their skills into the new aircraft while it was under construction at Hinkler's house. Farmer Stride permitted Hinkler to use his field for taxying tests as the Ibis neared completion. Hinkler cut a hedge at the bottom of his garden and put boards across a ditch to obtain access to the field. The completed aircraft was later towed to Hamble for flight testing for the aviation press.

Household pets included the marmoset that was given to Hinkler in Brazil and which he carried with him in the Puss Moth aircraft across the South Atlantic. It did not survive long into 1932. Earlier pets included Rufus, a Scotch terrier that did much travelling in the little Willys, and there was also Mickey, a cat. This was the famous threelegged cat for which Hinkler built a splint leg after it was caught in a trap. Mickey out-survived Hinkler. It was being looked after by Farmer Stride during the period of Hinkler's disappearance.

Bert Hinkler seems to have found his relaxation in practical pursuits rather than games. At one time he became a little concerned about his weight and rigged up a bar on a tree on which he performed various twists and turnovers. Another exercise he enjoyed was occasionally stroking a golf ball in the field owned by Farmer Stride. Hinkler owned axes and he used these expertly in producing the fuel for the household log fire. Around the house

Dr. Alberto Droandi, left, with representatives of the Australian and British Embassies at the inauguration by the President of the Italian Senate, Sen. Amintore Fanfani, of the Hinkler Memorial on Pratomagno in September 1968.

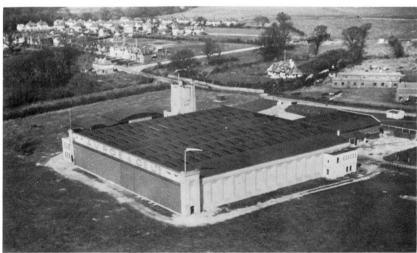

*Reg Hooker*

The Avro experimental establishment at Hamble. The small landing ground at the back of the works led to Southampton Water, lower left corner.

there was a field of natural grass and cutting this with a sickle and a scythe provided exercise.

When the Avro factory closed and Hamble Aerodrome became the headquarters of Air Service Training in April 1931, many of the old Avro staff left the area. The "new" companies were actually continuing under a common ownership, and Fred Bevis managed to complete fifty years of service with the same employer as a transport officer. But he was an exception. All the former Avro staff took a keen and personal interest in Hinkler's achievements when they read of them in the newspapers, but the world moved on and none had any direct contact with him after Avro closed its experimental establishment at Hamble and centred its activity at Manchester.

When Steve Brogden commenced his attempt to locate former Avro employees, the task was enough to daunt the most ambitious. He undertook it out of the same sense of loyalty that had stood him in good stead throughout his working life. Despite having had a variety of jobs, all the changes he made were a case of self-propulsion and never once was he sacked. He brought the task to completion and thereby preserved a unique record of the activities of a famous Australian far from home. At a later date he played an important support role in the preservation of Bert Hinkler's home Mon Repos, at Thornhill, when a plaque was placed on the site in 1974.

While Steve Brogden was hard at work on his task in Britain, he had a counterpart—though unknown to him—in Italy. There Dr. A. M. Droandi of the Ente Provinciale per il Turismo in Arezzo was ensuring that Hinkler's memory would not fade in the mountainous region where ended the famous aviator's flying career. Alberto Droandi had received his inspiration for this task when only twelve years of age. Hinkler's crash at that time remained one of the most indelible impressions of his boyhood. During World War II the fine memorial to Hinkler on the mountain crest directly above the crash site had been destroyed by partisans. Dr. Droandi was responsible for the erection of a new memorial to Hinkler on the summit of Pratomagno in 1968. Such ventures are by no means as easily accomplished as sometimes might appear. The president of the Italian Senate, Sen. Amintore Fanfani, inaugurated the memorial on 1 September 1968 in the presence of the

Australian ambassador, Mr. W. Crocker. Before his retirement from public duty, Dr. Droandi carried out further important Hinkler projects on which he expended much personal effort. Speaking different languages, but with a common objective, these two men—Steve Brogden of England and Dr. Alberto Droandi of Italy—both played honoured roles in preserving the Hinkler story.*

In Bert Hinkler's log book of long-standing personal friendships the name of Steve Brogden must appear very close to the top of the list. In spite of increasing age he maintained his enthusiasm over many years.

It is entirely appropriate that Dr. Alberto Droandi of Italy should share a place on that same first page, for both he and Steve Brogden did so much, each in his own way and in his own country, to ensure that Bert Hinkler's name was not forgotten.

*A photograph of Dr. Droandi appears on page 55.

# *Appendix 3*

# THE SAVING OF HINKLER'S HOUSE

The discovery of the log book of Hinkler's 1928 flight to Australia in the wing stub of the Ibis attracted press attention in England and Australia in 1953. Hinkler's home at Thornhill had become council property. Nancy was living with her daughter in South Africa. The Ibis was in a shed on the property where it had remained since Hinkler's death.

The Thornhill area saw considerable development after the end of World War II and the rural atmosphere disappeared. Modern buildings arose on nearby properties and Hinkler's house eventually came to be seen by the Southampton Council as out of style. It was very much in danger of being pulled down but received a reprieve because of its sound construction.

In order to ensure that the historic significance of the site was not overlooked, an approach was made to the Southampton Council by the author in 1973 for the purpose of placing a plaque on the property. Two elderly, but still energetic, friends of Bert Hinkler—Steve Brogden and Jim Laver—were anxious that this should be done. They later called on the council seeking to expedite a favourable decision. It had been hoped to time the plaque unveiling to coincide with a Hinkler Air Race taking place in Australia on 15 June 1974, but time passed until finally it appeared the opportunity would slip away. Fortunately, at the crucial moment, Kevin Lindeberg of Maryborough, a Queensland city 110 kilometres from Bundaberg, decided to make a private visit to England and, on hearing what was planned, he undertook to oversee arrangements. Leaving Brisbane in mid-May 1974, he carried with him a complete set of instructions that ensured the coordination of all parties in a successful project. On 23 May approval for the plaque to be placed was given by the Southampton Council, and he cabled this information to Brisbane. The plaque makers in Brisbane, with the layout prepared in advance, swung into action immediately. Bert Hinkler's sister Queenie prepared an unveiling cloth bearing the names of Brisbane, Bundaberg, Arezzo, and Southampton; skilled woodworker Pat Quinn of the Queensland Museum staff prepared a wooden case for the plaque, fittings, and unveiling cloth, and Qantas flew the boxed plaque to London for special delivery at a handover ceremony. Invitations had also been readied. In Southampton members of the Institute of Sound and Vibration Research gave total on-the-ground support, and the school at Thornhill, which depicts a biplane in its school badge as a tribute to Hinkler, provided assistance. The result was that on 15 June 1974, a very pleasant ceremony, which was attended by a number of aviation personnel from the old Avro days at Hamble, was held in the surrounds of Hinkler's house. Rowland Bound and Jim Laver addressed the gathering and reminisced on the Hinkler years. In Queensland, the air race proceeded as planned on the same date, and the dual tribute was completed successfully.

Within a few years it became clear that the Southampton Council was still intent on demolishing Hinkler's house and rebuilding on the site. Having been initiated into Hinkler matters through involvement with the plaque, and a subsequent visit to Italy, Kevin Lindeberg, temporarily resident in England, resolved to wage a one-man war to save the house and prevent its demolition. He sent letters to newspapers and various authorities throughout Australia and England. The *London Australian Monthly* featured his campaign. Letters began to arrive at the offices of the Southampton Council deploring its intentions. Demolition was stayed—temporarily. Lindeberg's campaign continued for four years, from 1979 through 1982. The council activity had been precipitated by the family in residence having applied to purchase the house. This served to bring the issue to a head. Late in 1982 it became clear that the plan to demolish the house would not be much longer delayed.

Lex Rowland (left), who suggested in late 1982 that Hinkler's house be obtained from Southampton and rebuilt in Bundaberg, with Kevin Lindeberg, who had previously campaigned in England for several years and saved the house from premature destruction. They were photographed together on the jubilant day in 1984 when the house was opened in Bundaberg.                    *M. Iso-Heiniemi*

Former Avro staff from Hamble at the plaque unveiling at Hinkler's home in Southampton in June, 1974. L. to R.: Bill Roe, Rowland Bound, Archie Blizard, Steve Brogden, Jim Laver, Jack Chouls, Pete Capon, and Fred Taylor.

*G. A. Cull*

Rowland Bound, Hinkler's partner in the Ibis project in 1929–30, addresses the guests at the plaque unveiling. About seventy guests attended the ceremony.

In Bundaberg, Hinkler's home town, there had always been a great desire to secure mementos of Hinkler, but know-how and finance alike had both been lacking. At this same time, late 1982, an idea was mooted in Bundaberg of obtaining Bert Hinkler's Thornhill home and reerecting it in that city as a special project to mark the Bicentenary of Australia, due in 1988. The imaginative proposal came from a Bundaberg citizen, Lex Rowland, who shared a common birth date—8 December—with Bert Hinkler and Bert's sister Queenie. Lindeberg was contacted by a member of the Hinkler family and agreed to assist. Early in 1983 he visited Southampton and, by invitation, addressed the council. It was fitting that this took place on 26 January—Australia Day. It marked the virtual end of his campaigning, for the need for it had passed. The Southampton Council received clear indications from other sources of growing support for the project. It had captured the imagination. Destruction was stayed for six months. The Bundaberg plan received wide acceptance and support in Australia, and the success of the transfer scheme was assured. Though very belated indeed in moving on Hinkler matters, Bundaberg thereafter did very well. A team went to England and systematically dismembered the house, readying it for shipment to Australia. The rebuilding of the house attracted considerable press coverage.

The result is that Hinkler's Thornhill home stands today on the crest of the hill overlooking the lagoons in Bundaberg where young Bertie Hinkler, nicknamed Spondulix by his friends, studied ibises as a boy and dreamed his dreams of flight. Hinkler House has proved itself one of the finest tourist attractions in Australia, and is an impressive tribute to one of the greatest of Australia's pioneering aviators. The plaque set in place in Southampton in 1974 in the presence of Hinkler's friends has been preserved. Still intact in the plinth provided by the staff of Southampton University, it occupies a position beside the house that it helped save for posterity.

# Appendix 4

# BERT HINKLER'S FLYING MACHINES

Six flying machines have a direct personal connection with Hinkler. Two of these were gliders that he built as a youth. The first glider was of fairly elementary construction and he tended later to disregard it, though photographic evidence proves that it flew. The second was of a higher degree of development and approached the status of an "engineless aeroplane." This was flown on Mon Repos Beach, near Bundaberg, in April 1912. Hinkler had been greatly impressed by Bleriot's flight across the Channel in a monoplane in 1909, and so had chosen the monoplane design, rather than the biplane, as the basis for his glider work. This called for individual resourcefulness, as his friends in the Aerial League in Brisbane were concentrating on biplane gliders.

A portion of Bert Hinkler's second glider survives, and a replica has been made and is displayed in Bundaberg.

The first aeroplane that Hinkler was personally connected with was the Bleriot owned by Wizard Stone, and this made flights—and crashes—in Australia and New Zealand in 1912 and 1913. Making repairs to the Bleriot taxed Hinkler's skill, but he was equal to the task. After the employment with Stone was at an end, Hinkler returned to Bundaberg before making his way to England. On his arrival there at Easter 1914 Hinkler found work with the Sopwith company, where he became familiar with the different types of aircraft constructed by the company.

While flying on raids in a DH4 with the Canadian lieutenant C. B. Sproatt, Hinkler had his first opportunity to handle an aeroplane in the air, but it was not until after the 1914–18 war that Hinkler had a flying machine he could call his own. This was the

Avro Baby in which he made the London-Turin flight of 31 May 1920 and the Sydney to Bundaberg flight in April 1921. The latter was an Australian nonstop long-distance record that stood for over six years. The Avro Baby was left in Australia when Hinkler returned to England in 1921, and after passing through the hands of several owners, it became the possession of J. J. Smith of Melbourne. He stored it under a house in the mid-1930s. In 1970 Jim Smith agreed to donate the aircraft to the Queensland Museum. By this time it had received several changes of registration markings—G-EACQ, G-AUCQ, and VH-UCQ. It was restored to flying condition by the Royal Queensland Aero Club, at the club's cost, as a tribute to Bert Hinkler, and has been displayed in the museum as G-EACQ since 1972. Although its permanent home is in Brisbane, the aircraft was on display for a period in Bundaberg in 1986, while "transiting" from the old museum site in North Brisbane to the new museum site in South Brisbane.

This aircraft, the Avro Baby, has a significance in aviation history quite independent of its famous owner. Designed by Roy Chadwick in 1919, it was the world's first practical light aeroplane.

A. V. Roe & Co. did not continue with the development of the Avro Baby type and thereby left the field of light aeroplane development to the de Havilland Company. De Havilland's Cirrus Moth, produced in 1925, won universal acclaim and met the long felt need for a light aeroplane suitable for use by the general public. The Avro Company responded in 1926 with an Avro Avian, a biplane of somewhat similar appearance and dimensions. The first of the Avro Avian type incorporated a number of features suggested by Hinkler himself. Eventually this aircraft became his private property and it was in the same machine, powered by an eighty-horsepower Cirrus engine, that he made his 1928 flight to Bundaberg and continued on around Australia to visit the other states. In September 1928, a heavy landing at Bundaberg damaged the wing spar and undercarriage. Bert Hinkler returned to England by ship soon after, and the Avian, which still bore its English registration G-EBOV, was left at Bundaberg. Subsequently, in May 1929, Hinkler donated the Avro Avian to the Queensland government for display in the Queensland Museum. The aircraft was temporarily repaired by Qantas maintenance staff and then placed on display at the Brisbane Exhibition of 1929. (In 1912 Hinkler's second glider had also been displayed at the Brisbane

174

Exhibition.) Soon afterwards the Avian was installed in flying position in the museum, the first photo of it in its new location appearing in the Brisbane press on 1 November 1929. It remained displayed in the same manner until 29 January 1986, when it was lowered to the floor and prepared for removal to the new museum. Its period on display coincided with the period from the Wall Street crash of 1929 to the Challenger disaster of 29 January 1986.* Hinkler's Avian now hangs in the museum at its new site in South Brisbane. An Australian art lover, Jack Manton, donated ten thousand dollars for refurbishment of the aircraft in 1986.

Construction of the Ibis amphibian occupied Hinkler's attention in 1929 after his return from Australia. The prototype, G-AAIS, was built and flew. Development, and promotion, of this project was partly the reason for Hinkler's presence in Canada and the U.S.A. in 1930 and 1931. The original design called for two engines set in tandem, one a tractor and one a pusher. Salmson engines were used for flying tests, but the intention was to replace them with a single more powerful engine, a two-hundred-horse-power Wolseley Viper. After Hinkler's death the Ibis remained in its shed on the property at Thornhill. Nancy Hinkler indicated it was available should Australian authorities wish to take possession of it, but the suggestion was not followed up. Eventually the Ibis reemerged in 1953, following Nancy's departure for South Africa, with newspaper reports suggesting it had become the property of a Mr. Stisted. After display at a Royal Aeronautical Society tea party in 1953 the Ibis disappeared from view and is said to have been destroyed in 1960 after Stisted's business passed into the hands of a new owner.

The final aeroplane owned by Hinkler was the Puss Moth he acquired in Canada in April 1931. It received the Canadian registration CF-APK, which it retained throughout its flying life. The Puss Moth was constructed by the de Havilland Company in England and erected in Canada. Hinkler incorporated features suitable to his own ideas. In this aircraft he made his tour through the Bahamas and the Caribbean, along the north coast of South America, and over the South Atlantic. It was in the same aircraft

*By coincidence a member of the Challenger crew, Dick Scobee, carried in his brief case in his locker a small piece of wood from Hinkler's 1912 glider. It was subsequently recovered from the Atlantic.

that he crashed on 7 January 1933. Very many parts of the wrecked machine were souvenired by mountain villagers who visited the crash site, and the remaining wreckage was destroyed at Pisa Airport, where it had been taken for examination. The Gipsy Major engine was retrieved from the mountainside and later sold to an Australian buyer. A Queensland grazier, Ted Hill, claims that for some years it powered his Genairco aircraft and that the origin of the engine was clearly attested in its log book. Unfortunately the Genairco deteriorated during wartime storage and was then sold. A Brisbane newspaper reported in the late 1940s that the engine had recently been purchased by the owner of a Tiger Moth. There are suggestions that the engine was still in use in Australia in the early 1980s, and there is no reason why this should not be so.

The flying helmet and gloves worn by Hinkler on his final flight are displayed in the Queensland Museum, together with the clock from the crashed aircraft.

In summary, of the six flying machines that have a direct connection with Hinkler, two survive—the Avro Baby and the Avro Avian. Remnants of a third—his 1912 glider—also are preserved, and a full replica has been built. Some small items from his Puss Moth, such as the dashboard clock and one or two mechanical parts, are in the Queensland Museum. The possibility exists that the Gipsy Major engine of this aircraft also still survives in Australia. Of the remaining two flying machines—Hinkler's first glider and the Ibis amphibian—there are no surviving fragments, as far as is known. However, in 1988, Bundaberg undertook a project to build a copy of the Ibis for display in conjunction with Hinkler House. The visual impression created by such a copy differs little if at all from the impression an onlooker would have received from the original. The atmosphere of the Hinkler pioneer flying era is more than modestly served by the wide range of flying and other tangible reminders available for public viewing.

# Bert Hinkler's Flying Machines

*F. A. Palm*

Glider 1 in flight. Ropes attached to the framework enabled Hinkler's youthful friends to pull the glider along the beach to create the conditions necessary for lift and also to retain some control should this be necessary when the machine took to the air.

*Len Cave*

Avro Avian G-EBOV incorporated some design features suggested by Hinkler. The divided undercarriage spread as the wings were folded, thereby lowering the engine and making maintenance easier.

Glider No. 2 in flight. Commenced at end of 1911, it was flown by Hinkler in April 1912.

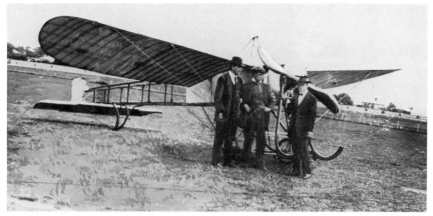

*T. P. O'Keeffe*

The American aviator Arthur Burr ("Wizard") Stone, centre, with his Bleriot aircraft in Brisbane in 1912. The figure on the right is Hinkler, whose ability came to Stone's notice in Bundaberg. Compare the stance with the photo of Hinkler beside the Ibis.

*R. Bound*

Rowland Bound (left) and Bert Hinkler ready for a test flight in the "Ibis" about the beginning of 1930. The aircraft was intended as an amphibian for Australian conditions. The name given the aircraft echoes Hinkler's efforts to construct gliders when a youth.

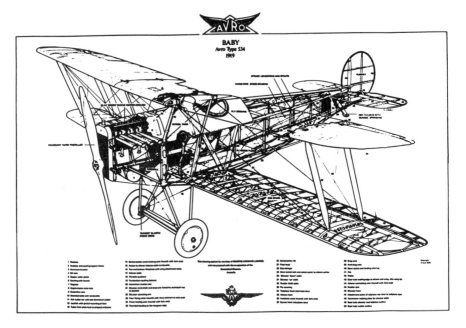

Technical illustration of the Avro Baby prepared by G. A. Cull. (Reproduced by kind permission.) The table below the aircraft is a numbered key to individual parts of the structure.

*Appendix 5*

# A PHOTOGRAPH ALBUM

# Hamble—Early Aircraft

The Avro Bison, a fleet spotter. Hinkler initially found difficulty landing this aircraft.
A cow is grazing just behind the farmer.

A La Cierva autogyro, 1927.                    *B. Boxall*

Roy Chadwick with the Avro
Baby.                    *M. Dove*

The Avro Aldershot on the small aerodrome at Hamble. In the form depicted it was powered by a 1000hp Napier Cub engine. An alternative version had a 650hp engine. Note size of the propeller. *Steve Brogden*

*The ultimate in Avro bomber aircraft design was reached with the Avro Lancaster, backbone of British bomber squadrons in World War 2. Like the "primitive" machines of the Hamble years depicted on this page, the Avro Lancaster was designed by Roy Chadwick.*

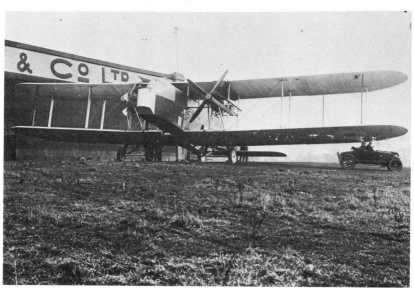

Avro Ava torpedo bomber. Hinkler is departing in his car. *B. Boxall*

# G. A. Lingham and the Savage family

At the tennis—Pauline left, Lingham right.

With young John Savage and the family car.

On board the *Mauretania*; apparently a shipboard farewell.

At a fancy dress gathering at the London Sketch Club. Lingham is on right in back row. Beside him is Jack Savage, and between them is Pauline Savage.

Farewelling Pauline and Jack Savage on the SS *Majestic*: Lingham and Allan J. Cameron (left) and Le Roy Van Patten of the Skywriting Corporation of America.

Below: Lingham (right) holidays with the Savage family, Birchington, 1924.

# Pratomagno—Aerial Views (1-4)

*PRATOMAGNO 1*

A—Croce di Pratomagno
B—Summit of Pratomagno
C—Mountain road built in 1970s
D—Wreckage found

*Arezzo Aero Club, 1974*

1. The view is from the Casentino side of the mountains across Varco di Castlefranco to Pratomagno. Hinkler's aircraft, lacking power, approached the crash site over the mountain slope from bottom right hand corner, where the mountainside falls steeply.

# Pratomagno—Aerial Views

A—Croce di Pratomagno 1591m (5220 ft.)
B—Summit of Pratomagno 1593m (5226 ft.)
C—1933 memorial above crash site 1516m (4973 ft.)
D—Wreckage found 1332m (4370 ft.)

*Arezzo Aero Club, 1974*

2. A view directly into the crash site on the Casentino side. The main wreckage was found at point D. Hinkler's body lay on the Prato alle Vacche, the small cleared area to the left of the crash site, at an altitude of 1330m. The wreckage pointed toward the bottom left hand corner of the photo.

A—Pratomagno
B—Wreck site
C—Hinkler's line of flight over Valdarno
D—Diversion over the Hill of the Wolf

*Arezzo Aero Club, 1974*

3. Looking from the Casentino side of the mountains into the "saucer" in which the wreckage was found. Viewed from the Florence end of the mountain toward the south. The wreck site represents a diversion from Hinkler's intended flight path over Valdarno.

A—Croce di Pratomagno
B—Summit of Pratomagno
C—Point of impact

*Arezzo Aero Club, 1974*

4. Hinkler's line of approach was from bottom right hand corner of photograph—from the northwest to southeast—as assessed by the Italian Air Force reserve officer Giuseppe Ghedini after viewing the wreckage on 28 April 1933. Ghedini also concluded that Hinkler's crash was not the result of a collision with the mountain face, a fact quite apparent from this aerial photograph.

The wrecked aircraft viewed from tail to engine. Note the tree trunk behind the tail and the encompassing mountainside. A similar photograph appeared in the Australian publication *Smith's Weekly* on 5 September 1936. The object on the rudder is Hinkler's left shoe.

# Pratomagno—Propeller Recovery

Italian Air Force recovery squad at Pratomagno, 2 May 1933

A squad of six members of the Italian Air Force, including a corporal, assisted Captain Gabrielli of Pisa Airport during the recovery of the wreckage from Pratomagno on 2 May 1933. The propeller hub appears to have been disassembled by squad members numbered 1 and 2. They may have observed significant features. It is possible that mementos were taken and that some members of the squad still survive. (Note: The villager seated nearest camera is holding the piece of cowling which formerly bore the name "Karohi.")

## Propeller Hub Assembly Structure

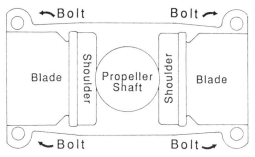

The metal hub plates are structured to fit tightly over the shoulders and inner sections of the blades and around the propeller shaft. Bolts and clamping rings secure the hub plates in position.

The clamping rings on Hinkler's propeller hub were double-bolted. This single-bolt type includes bolt, nut, cotter pin, clevis pin, and washer.

The propeller of Hinkler's Puss Moth, with hub plates bolted in place.

The blade recovered from the crash site. Subsequently displayed at Strada-in-Casentino, it was lost during World War 2.

# The Mountaintop Memorial

On 17 September 1933 the memorial to Hinkler erected by the Arezzo Aero Club was inaugurated on the mountaintop overlooking the crash site. Mules, some of which may be seen silhouetted, transported the official party to the site.

# Where Hinkler Was Found

Left. The spot where Hinkler's body lay was initially marked by a rough wooden cross. This was later replaced by a cross made from the aircraft's struts.

Right. A photo taken by the author during the 1983 commemoration activities on Pratomagno. Aladino Fabbrini (left), who watched over the body fifty years before, joins with Australian Kevin Lindeberg in placing a wreath on the spot where the body of Bert Hinkler was found.

The scene at Hinkler's graveside in the Florence cemetery at the conclusion of the fiftieth-anniversary memorial service in April 1983. The duke of Aosta faces the camera in the group at right. In the next group of three, also facing the camera, is the Australian ambassador. The author is at the extreme left of the assembly in conversation with the Anglican bishop who conducted the service. The day's events were a cause for nostalgia for the bishop, who recalled that he had been preparing for his own ordination at the time Hinkler was missing. A simple cross stands above Bert Hinkler's grave at the left. The grave is adorned with wreaths, partly obscured, at its head and foot.